47 THINGS YOU Can Do For The ENVIRONMENT

First published in 2012 by Zest Books
35 Stillman Street, Suite 121, San Francisco, CA 94107
www.zestbooks.net
Created and produced by Zest Books, San Francisco, CA

© 2012 by Zest Books LLC

Typeset in Sabon and Bureau Agency
Teen Nonfiction / Science & Nature / Environmental Conservation & Protection

Library of Congress Control Number: 2011931492

ISBN-13: 978-0-9827322-1-2
ISBN-10: 0-9827322-1-X

CREDITS
EDITORIAL DIRECTOR/BOOK EDITOR: Karen Macklin
CREATIVE DIRECTOR: Hallie Warshaw
ART DIRECTOR/COVER DESIGN: Tanya Napier
ILLUSTRATOR: Aaron Leighton
MANAGING EDITOR: Pam McElroy
RESEARCH EDITOR: Nikki Roddy
ADDITIONAL RESEARCH: Erika Stalder and Karen Macklin
PRODUCTION EDITORS: Sarah Wildfang and Pam McElroy

ADVISORS
ENVIRONMENTAL ADVISOR: Jill Buck, founder of Go Green Initiative
TEEN ADVISORS: Carolyn Hou, Maxfield J. Peterson, Joe Pinsker, Hannah Shr

Manufactured in China
LEO 10 9 8 7 6 5 4 3 2 1
4500322488

 This book was printed on paper using 50 percent recycled materials.

47 THINGS YOU Can Do For The ENVIRONMENT

Lexi Petronis

with Environmental Consultant Jill Buck, Founder of Go Green Initiative

Ever since I was a little kid, I have always loved our environment and felt strongly about protecting it. But I realized, about 10 years ago, that we were not doing enough to protect it. My biggest gripe was that the schools my kids went to were doing very little to teach students how to be good environmental stewards. I noticed that there were recyclables in every trash can, that energy and paper were being majorly wasted, and that "environmental education" boiled down to a silly puppet show about recycling on Earth Day. The teachers and parents were basically teaching the students what *not* to do. I knew there had to be a better way.

So, in 2002, I founded the Go Green Initiative, an all-inclusive environmental action plan that helps schools measure and reduce their environmental footprint. The initiative has since been adopted by schools across the United States and in 44 countries around the world. Because of this initiative, schools all over are greener, cleaner places. But there is still a lot of work to be done, and much of it is up to you.

47 Things You Can Do for the Environment is a great place to start. Your generation is one that values integrity, curiosity, and progressive thinking, and this book will help you create a lifestyle that reflects those values. By offering simple, yet meaningful ways to protect the environment on a daily basis, this book bridges the gap between Earth Day and every day.

My greatest hope is that this book will end up in the hands of millions of young people who will use it as a gateway into a new age in which we learn to treat the Earth as a precious place to be treaded gently upon, and handed down from one generation to the next.

There's no doubt about it, our environment is in crisis. Everywhere you go, people are talking about it: how the earth is warming up as a result of too much carbon dioxide in the air and too few trees left to absorb it, how oil-drilling is ruining natural habitats, how trash is overflowing into our waterways, and how chemicals used in various products are making people and wildlife sick. Ugh.

You *know* the planet is in trouble. The question is: What can you do about it? Go out and buy a brand new $30,000 hybrid car? Persuade all of the health clubs in your town to install low-flow showerheads and toilets? Revamp your entire house to operate on solar heat? Come on—you know better than anyone that this kind of stuff is hardly a reality for most high school kids. But what's the point of mulling over what you *can't* do, when there is so much that you *can* do?

You don't have to run out tomorrow and build a car that runs on vegetable oil, or ship out to South America to save the rain forests. You just have to get informed and start making small changes, one at a time. Decisions to shop, drive, and even party differently can have a huge and positive impact on the health of the earth. That's what *47 Things* is about.

In this book, you'll find tons of *real* things that teens can do to make a difference. Some things are as easy as eating less meat, planning a green date, or learning to shop vintage. Others are more involved, like hosting a green film festival for friends, creating an environmental task force at school, or going on an eco-adventure to gain a deeper love and appreciation for this beautiful spinning rock we call home.

Why teens? you might ask. The answer is simple. You're strong, creative, and motivated. You're doers and dreamers. And you're also the ones who will inherit the planet. If change is going to happen, it has to start with you.

47 Things You Can Do...

ONE: At Home [12]

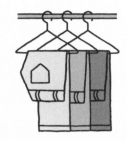

TWO: With Your Lifestyle [30]

47 Things You Can Do...

FIVE: While Shopping [58]

SIX: When Traveling [70]

1 Get a Clean Shave

Shaving is a big deal. For guys, the first shave is a whole rite of passage, signifying the transformation from boy to man. And the way guys grow out their facial hair, from goatee to sideburns, is a big part of expressing their personality. For girls, shaving means the difference between wearing that new skirt or throwing on those old jeans again. And when bikini time comes around, it's like half of a girl's beauty regimen! But shaving also takes its toll on the environment. That doesn't mean you should become a hairy-legged hippie chick or a bristly mountain man. Just take your hair removal to a greener level.

How to Do It

A lot of people use disposable razors when they shave—you know the kind that you use for a week or two and then have to throw away because they are all nasty and dull? Most disposable razors are not recyclable. You might think that the number of razors per year that you go through is insignificant, but it is estimated that about 2 billion disposable razors are thrown away every year in the US. The best and easiest alternative to all of this waste is to buy a long-lasting permanent razor with refillable blades. And depending on how much your razor and blades cost, this move may also save you some money over time.

Extra Tips

- Sharpen refillable blades with a razor sharpener, which can significantly reduce the number of blades you use.

- Use soap and water instead of shaving cream; soap comes with less packaging, and shaving cream containers are not always easy to recycle.

- Consider buying 100 percent recycled and recyclable razors.

A Sweet Way to Remove It

It's hard to decide what the most ecological form of hair removal is because so little research has been done on the environmental effects of things like waxing and depilatories. Both do employ the use of potentially toxic substances (especially depilatories), but there's still no conclusive evidence that suggests those substances are hurting our environment. Still, for a natural alternative, give body sugaring a try. It's like waxing, except you can use a natural mixture of sugar, water, and lemon. Look online for a complete recipe.

2 Put the Spin Cycle on Pause

Stop throwing your clothes into the hamper. That isn't to say you should throw them on the floor—the laundry lords in your house definitely wouldn't appreciate that. But not every item of clothing that you wear needs to get washed *every* time you wear it.

Washing just one load of laundry in a standard top-loading washing machine consumes about 40 gallons of water, so the less laundry you do, the better. Besides, washing less often will actually benefit some of your clothes.

Jeans, for instance, will last longer if you wash them less. Of course, no one's saying you have to go around wrinkly and stinky. Luckily, there are alternatives to washing that still keep your clothes looking (and smelling!) fresh.

How to Do It

To cut down on all that laundering, you need to extend the "clean" life of your clothes. The number one rule to remember: Hang everything up after taking it off (including pants). Letting used clothes air out for a bit helps to keep them fresh; when they're all smooshed up in a pile, they get wrinkled and smelly. You can also wear clothing that doesn't have direct contact with your skin—like sweaters or jackets—again and again, unless you acciden-

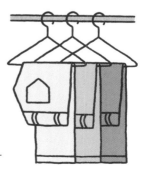

tally dropped a plate of spaghetti down the front. And use the same towel for an entire week, if not longer. Your body is clean when it gets out of the shower!

When you do get mustard on your shirt or a little blood on your collar from shaving, hand wash the spot with cold water. You'll avoid throwing the whole piece of clothing into the wash again (and have a better chance of getting the stain out).

Only run the washer when you've got a full load of clothes. That means you may have to include laundry from other members of your family to get a full load of whites, but a little teamwork and collaboration can keep your laundry eco-friendly.

Finally, if there are one or two items of clothing you want to wash, there's no need to do an entire load. Just wash those items by hand and hang them to dry.

At the Laundromat

If you help your parents take clothes to a laundromat, help them choose one with front-loading washers; they tumble clothes through a smaller pool of water (up to 50 percent less or 20 gallons less!).

3 Get Shower Power

The average American uses 80 to 100 gallons of water per day. To really process that, imagine emptying 100 1-gallon cartons of milk into an enormous bucket. That's a lot of H_2O! So, why should you care? One reason is that it takes a serious amount of **energy** to replenish, pump, and clean our water.

But there's also only so much water in the world. If we use up or pollute water at a speedier rate than it's being replenished, we're in trouble. The United States, unlike many countries, is lucky enough to have clean, running water, but it won't always be like that if we don't get wise and start conserving. In fact, due to population growth, **global warming**, and overconsumption, we may be facing the possibility of a serious water shortage in the next few years if we don't do something about it. There are so many easy ways to **conserve** water, and you can start in the shower.

How to Do It

1. **Shower with a water-saving showerhead (instead of bathing in a tub).** If you compare the amount of water used in a 10-minute shower (as little as 20 gallons, if using a water-saving shower head) versus that used in a bath (up to 70 gallons in a conventional bath tub), it's easy to see why showering is the champ in this department. But make sure you have a water-

saving showerhead! Old-school, conventional showerheads can waste as much water as a bath, depending on how long your showers last.

2. **Shower just once a day.** If you typically take two showers, cutting back to one per day could save thousands of gallons of water a year. Whether you shower in the morning to wake up or at night to clean up after soccer practice is up to you. And use bar soap instead of liquid soap—no bottles to throw away!

3. **Wash your hair every other day.** Do you have long hair? If so, washing it can add five minutes (at least 10 gallons of water) on to your shower every day. Washing your tresses less not only cuts down water consumption, but also protects the natural oils in your scalp.

4. **Talk to your parents about energy-saving water heaters.** Sure, you're probably not making any of the big financial decisions in your family, but if you make a big enough stink about our planetary needs, your folks will eventually start to listen (see pages 26–28).

Take a Green Bath

Sometimes we really *need* a bath. Maybe we are nursing an injury, or feeling grumpy, or just trying to beat cold winter blues. A bath once in a while is OK, if you're careful about not wasting water. Just fill the tub level high enough to cover you and keep you warm.

4 Color Your Hair Green

This doesn't mean literally dyeing your hair green—unless you want to. It simply means dyeing your hair in an eco-friendly way. Hair-dyeing is fun and can be the quickest, most dramatic way to achieve a new look. And, unlike some other methods of changing your look (like, say, getting a tattoo), the process is easy and painless, and the results are temporary.

But the problem is that most hair dye contains synthetic chemicals, and those have to go somewhere when you're done with them. The unused stuff from the kit (like the plastic gloves and the containers) goes into landfills where the chemicals can seep into the earth and taint the soil. The chemicals can also be harmful to your head—we're talking about scalp irritation, flaking, or even an itchy allergic reaction, called dermatitis. Whether you're going red, black, or violet, it's best to be green about it.

How to Do It

At home: Some herbal experts recommend tinting your hair with natural juices or teas—chamomile tea and lemons can brighten up blondes, while beet juice rinses add a hint of color to brunettes. Head to the health food store (check online for the closest one), where you can find hair coloring products that feature plant-derived or other natural ingredients, or look online for high-quality henna hair dyes, which are natural, and free of synthetic chemicals. The downside is that plant dyes don't last as long as the synthetic kinds, and they don't come in the same kinds of bold colors.

If you use any kind of dye with chemicals in it, you will have to properly dispose of the excess dye, bottles, and contaminated gloves, which some cities even consider a household hazardous waste. To get rid of it, see if your area has a special trash collection day where workers pick up household hazardous waste, or take it to a household hazardous waste facility yourself (see your city's website or visit earth911.com to find local places to go). You can also check with local hair salons to see what they do with their used dyes.

At the salon: Find a salon that aims to be environmentally friendly. Most salons use dyes made with toxic stuff—in abundance, but some greener salons use organic, plant-derived, and cruelty-free products as often as possible. Call local salons to see who's greenest. If there's an Aveda salon near you, that's a good bet. Aveda's demi-permanent (meaning it eventually washes out) dyes are made of 99 percent plant ingredients and their permanent dyes are made of more than 90 percent plant-derived ingredients.

5 Be a Natural Beauty

Beauty products may look pretty, but the multibillion dollar beauty industry can get ugly for the environment. How? Skin and hair products come in huge amounts of mostly **unrecyclable** packaging, and some of the ingredients can have negative effects on the environment. But you don't need to ditch your lipstick and aftershave. You just need to make some small changes to your shopping routine.

How to Do It

The next time you go to the drugstore in search of toiletries and cosmetics, consider the following.

1. **Packaging.** Avoid it whenever you can! Also, buy wooden makeup pencils instead of liquid ones encased in **plastic** since the wooden ones are likely to **decompose** and the plastic ones won't; and buy cosmetics that come in recyclable glass containers, instead of plastic tubes. If you support companies that use less or better packaging, more companies will follow suit.

2. **Unnatural ingredients.** The FDA does not yet have firm guidelines for products that are labeled "natural," but it does have a section on its site (fda.gov/cosmetics) that offers information about how cosmetics are (and aren't) regulated, what the FDA's stance on animal testing is, what ingredients are prohibited from being used, and what precautions you should take before using various cosmetics. And always read the ingredients!

When buying deodorants, perfumes, and colognes, beware of petroleum-derived chemicals, such as mineral oil, which are made with non-renewable resources like crude oil (think gasoline). Other ingredients that are potentially harmful are polycyclic musk HHCB (found in some perfume oils), and Benzophenone-3 (found in self-tanners and sunscreens). They can have potentially harmful reactions with our skin and, when washed from our bodies, they can have negative effects on our waterways and marine life.

3. **Containers.** Whenever possible, reuse them! Some green-minded pharmacies sell quality shampoos and lotions in bulk. Take your empty containers back to the store and refill them to save plastic.

To learn more, visit cosmeticsdatabase.org, a non-profit, non-partisan research organization that gives you the eco-scoop on all those unpronounceable ingredients. Also check out safecosmetics.org, which tells you about the cosmetic companies that hold themselves to higher ecological safety standards. And see the Green Resources section at the back of this book to learn about the Teens for Safe Cosmetics coalition.

Antiperspirants: Stinky for the Environment

Most antiperspirants have aluminum in them, the mining of which uses tons of energy. Use an aluminum-free deodorant without antiperspirant.

6 Bark Up the Right Tree

If you have a dog, you know the meaning of true love. Your dog is waiting for you every day when you come home, tail wagging, and mouth salivating. And while you'd never get up at the break of dawn to take out the trash, you would do it to walk your new puppy. Having a dog is great for your outlook on the environment because it teaches you to care about animals and nature (during park runs, yard play, and treks on snowy trails). But owning a dog—and especially walking a dog—also presents you with specific environmental responsibilities. So the next time you and Rex take a stroll or go for a beach run together, remember to walk him the green way.

How to Do It

To start, use a collar and leash for your pup that is made from organic material, like hemp, instead of the more commonly sold nylon. Nylon is durable—that's why people like it—but it produces the greenhouse gas nitrous oxide when being manufactured. Nylon also takes much longer to decompose than hemp because it is a synthetic fabric while hemp is simply made from a plant. Hemp is made to be quite durable these days, and hemp leashes can be found online through lots of companies like Earthdog (earthdog.com).

Once you're on your walk, keep your pup on his leash. Sure, you've successfully trained your beagle or pit bull to stay nearby most of the time, but that doesn't mean he's immune to the temptations of chasing squirrels in the bushes.

If you keep him on a leash, you can prevent him from accidentally digging up or destroying the natural habitat. Similarly, if you play frisbee or catch with your pooch, be sure not to throw the ball (or other toys) in the line of flowers and bushes. He wants that frisbee and he will go after it—no matter what lies in his way. Finally, if you have a backyard, scoop poop into biodegradable bags (which are generally made from corn products—and easily found online), then bury the bags in your yard. No, you can't put fecal waste like that in compost. That way the poop will decompose quickly on its own and not stick around for a lifetime in a plastic bag in the dump. (Note: Biodegradable bags must be buried; they won't biodegrade if they are just thrown out with the trash.) This is because they need to be in an aerobic environment (exposed to air) to decompose, as opposed to being trapped in a dump.

7 | Have a Green Christmas

If you celebrate Christmas, you may have realized that it's not the most **environmentally friendly** of holidays. There's a lot about it that screams "green"—trees, boughs of holly, Aunt Sarah's lime jello mold—but 'tis also the season for putting up shimmering **energy**-expending lights, chopping down precious trees, and buying lots of nonbiodegradable presents that are wrapped in **unrecycled** paper (which you may also be doing if you are celebrating Hanukkah, or any other holiday that celebrates with presents). But not to worry! With just a few simple adjustments, you can ensure a happy holiday for everyone, including the earth.

How to Do It

From your tree to what goes under it, these hints are sure to help.

Trees. Every year, Americans buy approximately 33 million real Christmas trees—and if every family throws its tree away, that's like cutting down whole forests! But **plastic** (or artificial) trees are equally problematic because they contain **non-biodegradable** plastics and possible metal toxins, like lead. Your best bet is to encourange your parents to buy either a burlap-balled or potted tree with the roots still attached. After decorating it inside your house and enjoying it during Christmas, you can replant it outside.

If you don't have space in your yard for a pine tree (remember, they get big!), see if you can donate it to your local parks department to replant it for you.

There are more than 4,000 Christmas Tree recycling programs all over the US. In many cities, there are also companies that grow Christmas trees in nurseries, rent them out to people for the month of December, and then replant them in their nurseries to continue growing. When the trees get too big, they get planted at city parks, on city streets, or in the wilderness. If you do go the regular cut-tree route, get one that was grown without pesticides. When the holidays are over, send it to be tree-cycled (the whole tree gets shredded into wood chips, which can be used for mulch).

Ornaments. Why buy ornaments when you can make your own? Look around your house and gather stuff you might toss out or give away and use it to create ornaments. Cut advertising leaflets into strips and loop them together to make a chain. Run a few glossy pages from a magazine through a shredder and make colorful tinsel. Or turn a burnt-out lightbulb upside down, paint on some eyes, and make it an art deco snowman. Make it a family activity!

Lights. Put up strands of twinkling LED lights, which use up to 90 percent less energy than regular incandescent string lights. Another idea is to get a timer that will shut off your lights automatically; that way, you don't accidentally let them burn into the wee hours.

Gifts. Give green! See page 64 for ideas.

8 Greenify Your House

You may not be the one buying the new hot water heater, but there's plenty you can do to turn your house into a green house, especially if you don't mind getting a little creative. Small changes can make a huge difference. Plus, your parents will be more apt to take your cause seriously if you're demonstrating some initiative.

How to Do It

Look around your house and identify all the places where energy is being wasted. Then find solutions. Below are a few ideas to get you started.

Problem: Your room is still cold even when the heat is pumping.

Solution: Make draft dodgers. You may have seen your grandparents stuff a towel under their door at some point to keep the cold out. This is similar—but slightly more sophisticated. Just take an old knee-high athletic sock, or two strips of any type of fabric sewn together to make a long tube with an open end, and decorate it as you wish. Then, stuff it with other socks or old T-shirts and secure it at the end so it stays closed. Now you're ready to put it underneath the door. Keep in mind that you may need to string two together for longer doors.

Problem: High energy bills are freaking out your parents.

Solution: To save energy (and money), trade your regular incandescent light bulbs for energy-efficient fluorescent bulbs (also called "compact fluorescent light bulbs" or "CFLs"), which use way less energy and last 4 to 10 times longer. It's even better if the light bulb you buy has earned an ENERGY STAR from the government. When you see this seal of approval on light bulbs it means they use about 75 percent less energy than regular bulbs!

Problem: You have paper messages scattered all over your house.

Solution: Put up a whiteboard and find some fun dry erase markers. When someone calls, you (or whoever) can write the message there instead of using pads of paper. No paper needed. Doodles encouraged.

Problem: The toilet water is a-wastin'.

Solution: Put a bottle half-filled with water and some sand or a few marbles in the toilet tank. Yeah, it sounds weird, but a weighted bottle nestled in the toilet tank (away from all the moving parts) will trick your toilet into using less water when it flushes—about 10 gallons less per day in a typical house.

Green Home Videos

Check out the Home Depot YouTube Channel or smartphone app for short, useful videos on reducing energy and water use around the house.

9 Involve the 'Rents

Y ou can't vote. You might not even be able to drive yet. But that doesn't mean you don't have any influence over your parents. Think back to the days when you were little. Your parents might have just left that injured bird outside, but you whimpered until they took it home to nurse it back to health. Maybe your mom would still be smoking cigarettes or your dad would still be eating bacon and cheese sandwiches for breakfast if you hadn't urged them to take better care of their bodies. Or maybe they followed your advice in a totally different way. The point is that parents, even if they sometimes act like they are too busy or not interested, ultimately *do* listen to what their kids are saying. And your folks are the ones with the real purchasing power (money!), so your input has a shot at not only influencing how they act, but also what they buy, which has a strong impact on the environment.

How to Do It

Plan a time for a green talk. Start by showing them a movie (see page 85 for ideas) about the environment, or just plan a dinner talk in which you know you'll have their attention. Tell them about the things you are learning in this book and what they can do to help the cause, and remind them that it's just as important to save natural resources for your future as it is to save money for your college education.

But, when you sit down to talk to your parents, you're most likely to meet resistance in two ways.

1. **They may not want to change their routines.** The idea of revamping one's life can be overwhelming, so you'll want to introduce them to green life slowly and gently. Break it down for them so they understand the whole story. (But don't patronize them, or your whole case will be thrown out.)

2. **They may be worried about the cost.** Switching over to a greener lifestyle can actually save your parents money right away, if they are learning to unplug stuff (see page 56), switch to **energy**-saving light bulbs (see page 27), and that sort of thing. But it can also be a bit more expensive at first if you are suggesting that they purchase big-ticket items like energy-saving appliances, hybrid cars, and low-flow toilets. Unless your parents are being featured in *Forbes* magazine on a regular basis, be prepared to discuss the issue of cost with them.

The best way to counter these obstacles is to know your stuff so you can present your parents with all the facts. Do research and be prepared to answer questions. Offer different energy-saving options so they feel like they have choices. If they get exasperated at your persistence, remind them that you had to inherit your determination and passion for humankind *somewhere*.

10 Eat Your Greens

If you haven't touched a hamburger since second grade after watching that PBS special about slaughterhouses, then you're on the green track. But if you're downing a Big Mac for lunch every day, then you might want to think twice about how much meat you're eating.

The country's livestock churns out 1 billion tons of animal manure (poop) each year, as well as a huge amount of animal gas (farts). The poop and gas produce nitrous oxides and green methane, which are actually way worse for the environment than carbon dioxide, the gas that cars emit. (Methane is 21 times more powerful at warming the earth's atmosphere than carbon dioxide.)

Eating animals comes with other environmental drawbacks, too. Livestock now use 30 percent of the earth's entire land surface. That means that the raising of animals overtakes and ruins a lot of forests and others types of land in some of the world's most beautiful places. Huge sections of the Amazon rain forest (as much as 70 percent) have been turned into pasture for animals that are being raised for slaughter, and into crops that feed those animals!

You don't need to be an animal lover to have motivation for eating a more vegetarian diet. And you don't even have to be a complete vegetarian to make an impact. You just have to eat *less* meat. One less hamburger a week adds up to 52 less hamburgers a year. Multiply that by the more than 300,000,000 people in our country and you can see what a huge difference it makes.

How to Do It

Eating a more vegetarian diet is easier than it sounds. It just means choosing a veggie burger over a hamburger, or a cheesy baked potato over a side of ribs. Many ethnic foods—like Indian, Thai, and Japanese—are loaded with vegetarian options, all of which are so flavorful you won't even miss the meat. You can also swap out meat for high-protein products like soy (tofu) or wheat gluten (seitan), which, when cooked properly, can take on a similar taste or texture to chicken or turkey.

Don't know where to start on the road to being an herbivore (or a more thoughtful omnivore)? Simply try one of your favorite meat dishes without the meat. For example, if you love burritos, nix the beef but keep everything else in it—beans, rice, cheese, tomatoes, lettuce, and salsa. You might find that it tastes just as good! Look online for great veggie recipes, and check out the smartphone apps from Allrecipes.com and Betty Crocker for tons of vegetarian main dishes!

11 Put Down the Bottle

Ever notice that bottled water has practically become an accessory? Whether it's from Vermont, France, or the Swiss Alps, bottled water has made its way into nearly everyone's hands, backpacks, and purses.

So, you're probably thinking—*What's the problem? Water is good for you, right?* Absolutely. It's the bottle that's the problem. Americans bought 8.45 billion gallons of bottled water in 2009, which cost about $10.6 billion. That's roughly 1,000 times the cost of tap water. And according to the public interest group Food & Water Watch, about 86 percent of empty water bottles get chucked in the trash (meaning they don't get **recycled**). Then there are the precious **fossil fuels** (in the form of gasoline) that we use when we transport cases of bottled water across the country—and sometimes farther!

Drinking lots of water is a great thing to do. It comes highly recommended by physicians, athletes, and supermodels as a way to stay healthy. So don't stop drinking water. Simply ditch the bottles.

How to Do It

Drink tap water whenever you can. In most places in the US, it's just as safe to drink as bottled water (you can check the safety of your local water by asking your water utility company for its annual water quality report). Tap water is even, in many cases, the smarter choice. For instance, tap water suppliers are required to test its water for chemical contaminants and share those results with the public, but bottled water companies are not. Some bottled water companies even get their water from public water sources. That's right, they bottle tap water!

If you're concerned about possible minor contaminants in tap water, or simply don't like how it tastes, buy a filter for your home. There are tons of affordable options, from the type that also serves as a pitcher, to a style that clamps onto your sink faucet. Also, invest in a reusable stainless steel container. Stainless steel containers are considered the safest ones because they don't contain BPA (Bisphenol A), a potentially harmful chemical produced during the production of plastic. Every morning, fill your container with tap water and keep refilling it throughout the day. If you have a strong preference for filtered water, ask your school to supply it to students so that they can fill up in between classes. Just remember: When using your own water bottle, make sure you wash it frequently with soap and hot water. Bacteria will accumulate if you don't.

And if you do ever wind up using a plastic beverage container, make sure you recycle it!

12 Check Your Carbon Footprint

Y ou know how the ground looks when it first snows? Everything looks so clean and nice until someone goes trudging through all that beautiful whiteness in big old boots. The more people are trudging through it, the nastier it gets. A carbon footprint isn't really so different. It's basically the amount of carbon dioxide each person contributes to the planet, whether from driving, traveling, eating, or shopping.

Everyone leaves carbon footprints, but the question is: How big are your boots? The first step (no pun intended) to reducing the size of your own footprint is to find out how big that footprint truly is.

How to Do It

Determining your carbon footprint is actually pretty easy, especially since there are many online calculators to help you do the math. Google "carbon footprint" to find them. Before you get started, you may need some of the info below about your house and your car (get your parents to fill in the blanks).

- The amount of kilowatt hours your home uses each month/year (find this on your monthly electric bill).
- The amount of miles that you've flown on an airplane in the past month and/or year.

- The amount of miles you drive (or get driven around) in a car each month and/or year. (You'll also need to know the make, model, and year of the car.)

Then, answer the questions on the site. After you've plugged in all of the information, you'll get a number. This number represents how much carbon dioxide you put into the environment every year—in tons. If your carbon footprint is high, make a goal to lower it (or "offset" it, as most of the websites say) by doing some of the things in this book. Then check it again next year … and see if your green initiatives have made a difference!

CALCULATE and OFFSET It!

While there are many websites that allow you to calculate your carbon footprint, terrapass.com does that *and* enables you to lower it. Through TerraPass, you can donate money to a project that is geared toward reducing greenhouse gas emissions (like a wind farm, for instance) and in so doing lessen the amount of CO_2 that you are pumping into the environment. If you want to check out your school's carbon footprint (and to see how it competes with that of other schools!), go to usa.zerochallenge.org.

13 Cans, Bottles, Paper, What?

I n 2009, Americans generated about 243 million tons of trash. That's ... a lot of junk. But, to our credit, we did recycle 61.3 million tons of it. In fact, our overall **recycling** rates have increased by 18 percent since 1990 and, since 1960, the amount of garbage sent to **landfills** has decreased by almost half (from 94 percent to 54 percent). That means that recycling is working, which is great news! And if we want it to work even better, it's important that we do it correctly.

When you throw things into the recycling bin, you probably get it right most of the time. But there are times when you might toss stuff in that doesn't belong. This can slow down the entire system, cause safety hazards for employees at recycling centers, and prevent other **recyclables** from getting, well, recycled. It's not just important to recycle, it's important to know what you can recycle and how to do it properly.

Keep Your Trash Clean

Before you put anything into the recycling bin, rinse it off. It is more difficult and expensive for recycling centers to process items that are covered in grease, oil, or food. Also remove staples, paperclips, and rubber bands.

How to Do It

Here are some recycling no-no's, but make sure to always read signs above recycling bins and check with your local recycling center to be certain of what you can and can't recycle at home.

Not Recyclable at Home	Why Not?	What to Do with It
Dry, empty, plastic bags or plastic bags filled with stuff	Empty plastic bags can get caught in the machinery at the recycling center, halting conveyor belts and holding up the whole show. Bags with items inside are even worse— they pose a safety hazard for recycling center employees who can't be sure what's inside.	Take your empty plastic bags to a plastic bag recycling bin. Many supermarket chains have these at the entrances. For more locations, check out plasticbagrecycling.org. And, no matter what's inside, don't put bags full of stuff into recycling bins; empty the bag, and recycle it separately. If you bring your own shopping bags to the grocery story, you'll eliminate your bag use all together!
Sneakers	The many different materials in them are hard to separate for recycling.	If they are in good condition, donate them to charity. Also, some athletic companies like Nike take used sneakers and turn them into playgrounds, running tracks, and gym floors.
Batteries	Batteries contain chemicals that, when burned or chucked into landfills, release toxins that can harm people and the environment.	Companies like Walgreens, CVS, RadioShack, and Staples frequently recycle old batteries for free. Go to earth911.com to see where to take them near you.
Some plastics	Plastics are numbered 1–7, and not all numbers can be recycled everywhere.	If you have plastics that can't be recycled at home (check your local recycling collector's website), set aside a bin for them and go to earth911.com, which will tell you where to take them.

14 Don't Toss That!

S o, you've finally gotten good at tossing bottles, cans, and newspapers into the big blue bin. Great! Now stop. No, just kidding. But before you toss something into the recycling bin, take a second to think: Do you really need to toss it out at all?

Recycling is fabulous, and you should always do it whenever you can. But it has its own costs that are good to know about. Here's how it works: Sanitation workers pick up your **recyclables** with their trucks. After the stuff gets to the recycling center, it's all sorted by the recycling center employees. Then, everything goes through different recycling processes. Glass and cans are separated, cleaned, and crushed before being shipped off to companies who'll melt them with other glass and cans to make new products. Paper is also separated, mixed with water to make a slurry, then rolled out to make new paper.

Recycling is actually pretty complex. And that's fine. But that also means it uses **energy**. So remember: Always recycle, unless you can reuse.

How to Do It

This is a chance to really get creative—and save some money! Have a bunch of old T-shirts with your favorite bands on them? Frame them and hang them on your walls instead of buying new art. Take your jeans with holes in the knees and remake them into shorts or skirts (or use those old T-shirts to patch them up). Use old bedroom posters to wrap gifts or design cards. Brainstorm with friends for more ideas or check out some websites that are all about turning old things into brand-new ones (such as recycle.co.uk).

And just because something breaks, doesn't mean you *have* to throw it out. Find a new home for it, repair it, repaint it, regift it, or reuse it. Your old stuff can take on a totally new life as something else, and you'll be surprised at the kinds of things you come up with.

Don't Throw Me Away!

Was	Can Be
an old shoebox	a new art supplies or makeup box
an old half-used spiral notebook	a new scorecard for Scrabble
an old shopping bag	a new gift bag for a friend's present
an old suitcase	a lounge pad for your cat or dog

15 Let No French Fry Go to Waste

Y<!-- dropcap -->ou may not always love cafeteria food, but it's still food and it's still a shame when it goes to waste.

The Environmental Protection Agency (EPA) says food left-overs—including those from school cafeterias—are the single-largest component of the waste stream by weight in the US. You've seen it happen—people tossing full cartons of chocolate milk, unopened bags of chips, and uneaten apples into the trash. Most schools also have excess food every day that they wind up tossing when students eat off-campus, bring lunch from home, or simply choose not to have lunch. That's a lot of food heading straight for the **dumps**. You'd think it would **decompose** there, but because of the **anaerobic** conditions (it sits in **plastic** bags and is not exposed to air) the food just releases the **greenhouse gas methane** into the atmosphere! And food waste is not just sucky for the environment—it's a shame for all of the hungry people who could really use that food. That's why it's a great idea to start a food donation program at your school: You'll stop food from ending up in **landfills** and also help the less fortunate in your area.

How to Do It

Starting a food donation program may take a lot of time and determination, but you can make it happen if you are persistent. Begin by approaching your favorite teacher, coach, or the head of your after-school club with your idea and ask them for support. Then, find out which faculty member handles the lunch program and go with your supporter to talk to them. Ask how much excess food your school cafeteria prepares and suggest sending it to food banks and other organizations in the area that accept prepared food. (But make sure you do some research beforehand so you're prepared to offer specific names of programs.) Some food banks accept only non-perishables, like canned goods and bags of potato chips, and others will be able to take more.

You will eventually have to bring your idea to the principal, and then to people beyond your school, like district officials. If your proposal gets put into action, congratulate yourself! Then, make sure that the school sets up a donation area in the cafeteria where students can put their unopened bottles of juice and bags of chips; also check that cafeteria staff know how to package up whatever has not been eaten according to the instructions of the food bank or organization.

Teach the School to Compost

Though you can't donate half-eaten food (gross!), you can teach the school to compost it if they don't already. Basically, a **compost** pile is a mixture of soil and decaying garbage (including food) that helps fertilize and condition the earth. Composting puts organic, **biodegradable** matter back into the soil and keeps it out of **landfills**. Some schools even sell their compost to local farmers so they can use it to grow better crops. Look online for helpful school composting sites.

16 Get the Right Stuff

When you were just starting school, the "right" supplies were the ones with Elmo or sports teams on them. Now, of course, you know it's not so much what your school supplies look like—it's what they're made of. Notebooks, binders, paper clips, pencils … your list of what you need is long, and that equals serious waste when you're done with all of it. But there are ways of getting eco-smart about your school supplies without resorting to taking notes on your hand.

How to Do It

Start by inspecting your backpack. Many packs are constructed of polyvinyl chloride (PVC) (or "vinyl"), a type of **plastic** that's often considered the most **toxic** because it consists of **chemicals** that are dangerous for the workers who make them, harmful to the people who use them, and toxic when burned for disposal. Because of its chemical makeup, PVC is not only hard to recycle, but it can be hazardous to recycle. And backpacks aren't the only thing made of PVC—the companies that make binders and folders go crazy with that stuff. To check if a product has PVC, see if the packaging has the number 3 or the letter "V" underneath the **recycling** symbol. You can also use your nose: PVC products have that plasticky smell, like the scent of a new shower curtain.

Now take a second to think about how many pens you have thrown out this year. Then multiply that by every student, office worker, and human being on the planet. Can you even imagine how many trash cans that would fill?

The answer: Buy refillable pens. Then, the only thing you need to trash is the refill.

As for everything else, buy stuff that has *already* been recycled. That means anything that is made with **post-consumer recycled** materials, from cardboard and **plastic** binders to special pencils made of post-consumer recycled materials (which range from old cafeteria lunch trays to shredded dollar bills!). This stuff is all available—you just need to read the labels.

Know Your Arrows

Remember to buy stuff that says both "recyclable," which means that it has the potential to be **recycled**, and "recycled," which means that it is *made* of the bottles, cans, and paper you've been recycling.

recyclable

recycled

Plastics By the Numbers

Most plastic containers have a number on them to help people sort them properly. Your local recycling plant, for instance, may only accept numbers 1,2, and 4 (the most easily recycled plastics) and not numbers 3, 5, 6, and 7 (which are either hard to recycle or totally unrecyclable). When recycling at home, check with your local recycling plant to see what numbers they accept and make their job easier by only tossing those plastics into your blue bin.

17 Cut to the Paper Chase

Paper is everywhere. You use it to write your essays, to work out your calculus proofs, and to pass notes to your friends. But do you ever really think about where it comes from?

We all know that paper is made from trees. But how does it go from being the mighty oak to the easy-to-tear, fragile sheet of paper? Here's the deal: After the trees are cut down, they're washed, debarked and cut into tiny little pieces. Then the wood chips are treated with **chemicals** that separate the usable wood fibers from the gluey part of the tree (the lignin) to make a soggy pulp. The pulp is cleaned, drained, and mixed with water. It's then pressed into sheets, coated to look glossy, and cut into pages. The process is obviously more complicated and scientific, but the basic point is that, between the trees and the **energy**, making new paper uses a lot of **natural resources** (like trees and **fossil fuels**) as well as **chemicals** (like chlorine) that are **toxic** to our air, water, and soil. To make matters worse, paper is the number one material that we throw away. For every 100 pounds of trash we throw away, 35 pounds is some kind of paper!

How to Do It

Recycling 1 ton of paper (about 220,000 sheets) saves 17 mature trees, 7,000 gallons of water, 3 cubic yards of **landfill** space, 2 barrels of oil, and 4,100 kilo-watt-hours of electricity—enough energy to power the average American home for five months! Of course, it's essential that you not only recycle but also *buy* products made of recycled paper (see page 43 for the icons to look for). Otherwise, the system doesn't work.

When purchasing products with recycled paper, you'll see two different kinds:

1. "Post-consumer" recycled paper is made from paper that has been used and recycled into new paper.

2. "Pre-consumer" recycled paper is made from unused, leftover scraps of paper that were cut at the paper mills, but were never actually used.

Post-consumer recycled paper is better because it takes fewer natural resources to produce. But even if you can only get your hands on the pre-consumer recycled kind, that's still better than buying brand-new pages.

Reuse!

One of the best things you can do is reuse paper before even tossing it into the recycling bin. Simply use the backs of old photocopies as scratch paper and print out your homework assignments on both sides of the paper.

18 Paint the Halls Green

If you are the creative type, you might find all of the scientific and statistical stuff related to the environment boring. That's probably one reason why some people tune out when it comes to learning about it—terms like "*chlorinated hydrocarbons*" and "*petroleum derivatives*" can be a little off-putting.

But it doesn't have to be all science-speak. You can promote the idea of green living to others by using your creativity. Are you a poet or an actor? Can you compose music? Whatever your art, you can make the environment your muse and get your message across in a unique way. Then, develop it into an event in which you can raise money for your cause.

How to Do It

Everyone has an environmental cause that's near and dear to their hearts. If you are a surfer, it might be protecting the beaches. If you love to go backpacking, you may be committed to preserving open spaces. Once you know your message, decide how you want to communicate it to the world.

- **Write and put on a play.** A play with an environmental bent doesn't have to be serious. On the contrary, it can be hilarious, inspiring, and artistic and still communicate a good message. Contact the outreach coordinator at your local community center or the manager of your school's performance space and recruit local actors to help you put it on.

- **Write and perform a song.** There's a reason commercials have jingles—snappy songs are hard to forget. But your ode to the environment can be something way more soulful. Practice what you preach by performing your masterpiece with acoustic instruments so you won't have to use electricity when you perform!

- **Paint a mural.** A mural is a big project, but one that's well worth the time. If you want to paint a mural on a private piece of property (like the outside wall of a local store), talk to the owners and/or managers of the building about your idea. Be specific and even provide sketches to help persuade them to let you do it. To get your work on public property (in a park or public school wall), contact your city's youth, public arts, or beautification committees to see what opportunities are available. In some cities, arts nonprofits like San Francisco's Precita Eyes and Philadelphia's Mural Arts Program specifically work with the city to create murals. Once your mural is done, organize a big opening day to draw people to publicize the new work.

- **Hold a reading.** If you have a way with words, write a poem or story about your cause, and ask other writer friends to do the same. Reserve a coffeehouse or local bookstore and have a public reading!

- **Write a blog.** Use a free blogging platform like WordPress, Tumblr, or Blogger to take your message to the masses. Incorporate videos, photos, and audio clips to offer a multimedia experience.

Take It to the Top

As a student, you probably feel like there are a lot of things going on at your school that you don't have much control over. In a way, you're right: It's not like you can go to the principal, demand that all kids be required to walk or bicycle to school or else face immediate expulsion. But you may have more control than you think. If you speak up about a problem that you feel is important, and especially if you propose a solution, school officials and teachers will likely listen.

How to Do It

You can try to make small changes on your own, but consider going a step further and form a student task force—there's power in numbers. Once you have a few fellow students to back you, come up with an agenda.

Where to start? Think about this: In the US, K-12 schools spend more on energy than on computers and textbooks combined. So, one of the first things you can campaign for is upping the efficiency of your school. Ask teachers and fellow students to turn off the lights in the classroom when not in use. In a typical school, lighting accounts for almost 30 percent of the electric bill, and you can be sure that leaving the lights on in empty rooms is contributing greatly to that percentage. Also, get the school to keep the room temperature regulated. Not only can overly heated and overly cooled classrooms make students uncomfortable while they're trying to learn, but it also wastes energy. A good rule of thumb is 68 degrees for heating in winter and, if you are lucky enough to have AC in your school, 78 degrees for cooling in summer. And keep classroom doors closed so the heat or cool air doesn't escape!

Recycling is also important. If your school already has a recycling program in place, ask if recycling bins can be moved to every classroom, the cafeteria, the library, even hallways—the more bins you have, the more likely people are to use them. If your school doesn't have a recycling program yet, start one! (See page 100 for tips on how.)

Another thing you can do is talk to your teachers or principal to see if they can offer extra credit to students who help. Offer to hold fundraisers to pay for bigger ticket items. What administration is going to say "no" to energy-efficient double-pane windows when you just raised the money to buy them?

Want More?

For more practical ideas on how to prevent waste and save energy in your school, go to epa.gov and ase.org and type "school" into the main search boxes. Also, check out the Go Green Initiative Planning Guide, a free environmental education program, at gogreeninitiative.org.

Feel the (Solar) Power

We're in an energy crisis, right? But check this out: In one hour, the sun radiates enough energy on Earth to meet the energy needs of everyone on the entire planet for a whole year! So, where's the crisis? Obviously, the problem is that we haven't figured out how to fully take advantage of the sun's energy. It's time to start. When thinking solar, those massive silver panels on top of houses usually come to mind, but restructuring the roof is a big project for a teenager. Instead, think about using solar rays to power all of the energy-sucking gadgets you use. Everything that you plug into a separate socket needs energy, which usually comes from facilities that burn nonrenewable natural resources, such as coal, to produce power. When you solar charge, the only thing you use is the sun's rays, which there is no shortage of.

How to Do It

Ditch those energy-sucking USB chargers that power the NiMH batteries housed in your iPod, cell phone, camera, and/or Wii for a portable solar charger like the Solio. Manufacturers also make solar backpacks and messenger bags that work double-time to hold your stuff *and* charge your gadgets.

When you need batteries, buy rechargeable batteries instead of the regular disposable alkaline batteries, and charge them with a universal solar battery charger. Even if rechargeable batteries cost a little more upfront, you'll be saving yourself money and helping the environment in the long run. You can also buy stuff that has solar panels so you don't need batteries at all. Ask about these types of products when you shop for new electronics.

How Solar Works

Even though solar power has just started to get mainstream, solar power is old news. It was 1883 when American inventor Charles Fritts developed the first photovoltaic cells (or solar cells). These cells, when grouped together, form a panel that captures light and then converts it to direct current (DC) electric power, which is then converted into alternating current (AC). This is the electrical energy that flows to your house and gadgets. Gloomy outside? Not to worry. New technology lets you "solar charge" from incandescent or fluorescent lamps when access to the sun is not available.

21 Save Your Cell

At least 75 percent of teens in the US, ages 12-17, have cell phones. This is great because it means you are all staying connected to each other and the world around you. But that also means that you're responsible for conscientiously disposing your phones. More than 130 million cell phones are tossed every year in the US, and it is estimated that only about 10 percent are ever recycled. Apart from the amount of landfill space these discarded devices take up, they also hold some dangerous stuff, such as arsenic and lead, which can leak into the ground, taint the soil and groundwater, destroy ecosystems, and poison wildlife and drinking water.

If you are going to throw away a cell phone, it's best for you to bring it to a place that accepts hazardous waste. (Some states have laws that actually prohibit you from tossing cell phones in with regular trash.) But even when you dispose of phones properly, there is a chance they may be shipped off to much poorer countries and burned there, sending toxic fumes into the air where innocent people have to inhale them. Not good. The best thing to do with cell phones is to donate, recycle, or resell them.

How to Do It

Your old cell phone may be a piece of junk to you, but there are many charities that think it is a little piece of solid gold—so donate it. Choose an organization that is equipped to accept cell phones, and the folks there will clear the information from your phone, making it ready for use by someone in need. Some places will give the phones to clients—say, a victim of domestic abuse who needs a way to make emergency calls, or a homeless person who is trying to get a job but can't do so without a phone.

Other charities may decide to resell your phone to a company who will buy it and then fix it up and sell it or recycle its parts. It's still a win-win situation. Your charity of choice makes money for its cause and the refurbishing company makes money for its business. For example, the teen-run charity Cell Phones for Soldiers collects old phones and sells them to ReCellular, a refurbishing company. Then, Cell Phones for Soldiers converts the cash it receives into calling cards for soldiers who are serving far away from their families. There are also businesses that will give you money for your old phone, depending on how old it is. Even cell phones that don't have any imaginable value can be resold or recycled. Just google "recycle" and "cell phone." You'll be surprised at how much comes up.

Where Does It Go?

To learn more about where our cell phones and other electronic waste often goes, go on cbsnews.com and search for the 60 Minutes video called, "The Electronic Wasteland."

22 Compute the Difference

There's no disputing that the computer is one of life's greatest inventions. Think about how often you use yours: for homework, to update your Facebook status, to watch TV shows you missed.

Now think how often you *don't* use your computer. Like when you talk to a friend on the phone, read a book, take a nap, or have dinner with your family. No one's online 24/7. But your computer may still be powered on while you're powered off. Idling computers suck up a lot of energy while they're busy doing, well, nothing. As we move forward into the Green Age, we have to start thinking about big ways to combat computer energy drain.

How to Do It

It sounds really basic, but simply shut down your computer. That doesn't mean to only turn the monitor off, but truly shut it down when you won't be on it for a long stretch. And take the plug out of the wall (see page 56). You might think it takes more energy to turn your computer on and off, but the small amount of energy used when it comes on is still less than the amount it uses when running for long periods of time. If you're going to be away for only a few minutes or even a few hours, simply power-down your computer into Sleep. That turns off the monitor while the computer takes a low-power snooze, but the hard drive will remember all of your open browser windows and documents. The machine wakes up quickly with a tap on the keyboard, bringing you right back to the screen you've been working on. If you have a PC, you can also use Hibernate, which powers down your computer (like Shut Down), but also saves an image of the files you are working on, so they will still be there when you boot up again. And remember to turn off your monitor when you're not at the computer so the screen isn't always burning energy.

When buying a new computer, get an ENERGY STAR-qualified computer; these are the most energy efficient computers you can buy. If all the computers in the US met ENERGY STAR requirements, the savings in energy costs would be more than $1.5 billion each year. Also, if possible, buy a laptop. Laptops use at least 50 percent less energy than desktop computers.

CALCULATE It!

You can calculate how much energy your computer saves when you use Sleep or Hibernate. For PCs, go to energystar.gov and for Macs, go to apple.com. Just search for "computer energy calculator" on both sites. To figure out how much energy your computer saves when you use sleep or hibernate mode, google "computer energy calculator."

23 Rewind and Unplug

You know that electronics drink up most of the power in a house. But did you know that, in the average home, 40 percent of the electricity used to power home electronics is consumed while the products are turned off? Doesn't that seem like a huge waste? But it's true. Every time you leave your cell phone charger plugged in after you've removed the actual cell phone, a constant stream of energy trickles out of the still-plugged-in charger. Now think of how many electronics you have that are plugged in right this second that aren't being used. Does your bedroom television need to be plugged in all day while you are at school? Does your family really need the AC unit plugged in during the winter?

Unplugging your appliances will go a long way in reducing energy waste, and it may even save money on the monthly energy bill—something that Mom and Dad will most definitely notice (in a good way).

How to Do It

Unplugging is pretty easy—you probably don't need a blow-by-blow on how to disconnect your cell phone charger from the wall. But it can get easier. Plug all the components of your computer, TV, or stereo into one power strip, which you can turn off with just one switch. (No need to unplug the power strip; it's made so that the electricity won't move through it if it is switched to "off.")

Also consider using a "smart" power strip, which senses when the electronics plugged into it are turned off and then switches off on its own.

Of course, it's fine to theorize about unplugging stuff, but it doesn't help unless we actually do it. And humans are very good at forgetting. That's why certain smartphones have apps that alert you when the battery is charged and should be removed from the power source. This is a great green move.

But until *all* of our electronics are talking to us, we need to remind ourselves to unplug them. If you are forgetful, try leaving yourself a note that you'll see every day before you leave for school, or program a daily reminder on your phone that reminds you to unplug.

Turn Out the Lights

It seems like a no-brainer, but people forget to do this when they walk out of a room, and it really makes a difference. You can also save energy during the day by studying in the sunniest room of the house, under a skylight, or next to a window. If your parents are willing to shell out some cash for the cause, you can even invest in motion-detecting lights that are only activated when you walk into the room.

24 BYOB (Bring Your Own Bag)

Isn't it funny that no matter what you buy in the store—a new CD, a stick of chocolate-flavored lip balm, or a bite-size external hard drive—you wind up with a **plastic** bag to take it home in? Before you can say, "No, thanks. I don't need a bag—this apple will fit in my pocket," your apple is packed for you and ready to go. Estimates of the number of plastic bags used around the world each year vary, from 100 billion to as many as 1 trillion, and it's really problematic for the earth. Most plastic bags are produced by using nonrenewable resources like **crude oil** and natural gas, and are made from polyethylene, which makes them **non-biodegradable**. They can be recycled, but must be taken to special places for that (see page 37). Otherwise, they end up getting trashed and contributing to **landfills** or, worse, flying around aimlessly, clogging **waterways**, getting stuck in plants and trees, getting caught in animals' throats, and even harming ocean life. It may be hard to stop using a car (even though we know it's so bad for the environment), but how easy is it to just stop using plastic bags?

Paper bags are marginally better because they are **biodegradable** and **recyclable**, but it's important to keep in mind all of the trees that need to get cut down so they can be made. Paper bag production also causes a ton of air and water pollution. So whether you're buying holiday gifts for friends (see page 64) or picking up new clothes (see page 62) at the mall, your best bet is to BYOB (bring your own bag).

How to Do It

You can just toss stuff—especially if it's already packaged—right in your backpack. For more delicate things, use a canvas bag designated specifically for shopping excursions. A canvas bag will tote everything from a pound of peaches to new Pumas. The best kinds of canvas bags are free. You know the kind: they come as gifts with magazine subscriptions, new gym memberships, and that sort of thing. You can also find funky ones for next to nothing at thrift stores and yard sales, or get more expensive versions at health food stores where they are sometimes made with organic cotton and/or come in foldable shapes that can be stuffed into a pocket and then pulled out and unfolded when needed. Just remember to put items in your bag *after* you've paid and the transaction is completely over and done with.

Bring Your Own Coffee Cup, Too!

If you are a big latte lover, keep a refillable, washable mug or thermos in your backpack so that whenever you hit your coffee joint of choice, you can whip it out. The bonuses: 1) You cut down on paper waste from the cup and the cardboard heat sleeve; and 2) Some cafés offer discounts and/or free refills when you provide your own cup.

25 Go Vintage

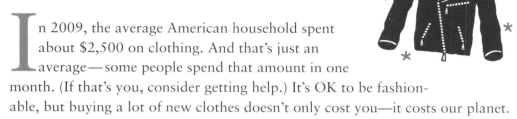

In 2009, the average American household spent about $2,500 on clothing. And that's just an average—some people spend that amount in one month. (If that's you, consider getting help.) It's OK to be fashionable, but buying a lot of new clothes doesn't only cost you—it costs our planet.

Manufacturing brand-new clothing is hard on the environment. One example of this is the process of making **synthetic** materials such as polyester, which requires a lot of **crude oil** and **energy,** and flushes all kinds of dangerous **chemicals** into the **water stream.** All those new clothes have to get to the stores to be sold—and that takes a huge amount of fuel. And once we've bought the clothes, the wasteful journey isn't even close to the end, because when we throw the clothing out, it contributes to **landfills**!

Of course, we can't just go naked. And though we can be more ecologically minded when we shop for new clothes (see page 62), it's even better to buy **recycled** clothing. If you've never ventured further into the world of secondhand clothing than your older siblings' hand-me-downs, you may think "recycled" or "second hand" is simply code for moth-eaten sweaters, stretched-out pairs of mom jeans, and stained sweatshirts. But lots of trendy secondhand clothing—aka vintage—is modern (even when it's classic), stylish, and already broken-in. And the best part is that vintage threads cost a fraction of what they would brand new.

How to Do It

Shopping vintage doesn't necessarily mean picking through bins at Goodwill. Many higher-scale vintage and consignment shops buy and sell only close-to-new name brand stuff. Others specialize in great finds from past decades, which is cool if you like retro style. And because everything is one-of-a-kind, there will be very little chance that someone at school will also be wearing your new top. If you're new to the whole vintage concept, consider these tricks of the trade.

- **Go regularly.** Vintage stores frequently refresh their inventories, so there may be new things in stock as often as every day (check with store managers for details).

- **Be open to making alterations.** You're getting stuff at such a discount that you can afford to have some minor alterations made if the perfect jeans end up being a couple of inches too long.

- **Get creative.** Secondhand shops are great places to look for unusual fabrics that can be cut apart and sewn into new things, or used as part of a Halloween costume.

- **Resell your own clothes.** Trade in the higher-end items in your wardrobe that you no longer wear for a few bucks or store credit. You won't make back the amount you initially spent on those now too-tight Sevens, but you'll get a little money and contribute to the save-the-planet cause.

26 Buy Green Threads

While the most eco-friendly shopping choice is to buy recycled clothes (see page 62), there are times when you just have to buy new. Maybe it's prom time and the vintage store in your neighborhood is seriously lacking cute dresses, or the only jeans that fit you at the used-clothing store are shot through with holes. If you are going to buy new clothes, buy ones that are eco-smart.

How to Do It

Buy clothing from companies that design with the environment in mind by using recycled materials or organic fabric. It's also important to simply read the small print. You might absolutely love that new skirt, but if it's made with artificial dye or polyester, it's probably harming the environment.

Researchers estimate that, because dyes have a hard time adhering to certain fabrics (like cotton), about half of the chemicals used in dyes end up in the environment via wastewater. If the dyes are artificial, they can harm aquatic ecosystems. So, one way to start shopping for eco-friendly threads is to buy clothing that's created with natural dyes (like indigo or logwood).

Also, buy clothes made with "e-fibers," or environmentally friendlier threads like hemp, chlorine-free wool and organic cotton. The most popular e-fiber is organic cotton, which is grown with little-to-no pesticides or synthetic fertilizers, as compared with commercial cotton. Once you buy your new clothes, take good care of them so you can wear them for a while—or at least swap (see page 82) or resell them (see page 61) when you grow tired of them. And hang dry them when possible to save on energy.

CALCULATE It!

You figured out your own carbon footprint on page 34. Want to see the carbon footprint of your clothing? Eco-conscious clothing brand Patagonia has devoted part of its website to calculating the eco-footprint of some of its products. To see this, go to patagonia.com/us/footprint.

Save Your Sole

You read on page 37 about Nike's program to use old sneakers to make playgrounds and running tracks. But did you know that some shoes are even made from recycled materials? Designers like Simple Shoes, Teva, Flat Tire Footwear, and Worn Again make shoe soles from old tires, shoe fabric out of recycled plastic bottles, and shoe uppers from old military jackets!

27 Give Green

It's your best friend's birthday, Father's Day, and your cousin's graduation all in one weekend. There's only one thing to do—buy gifts! And, as Americans, we do a lot of shopping. The average American spends around $700 during the Christmas season alone. Shopping, though, is not only hard on our wallets—it's hard on the environment. Why? Stuff contributes to waste. Look at the presents we buy. We often give people we love little trinkets that we think say "I'm thinking of you" but really say "Here's some more useless stuff." Most of it eventually gets tossed and ends up in our overflowing land-fills. And all of those gifts come with tons of wrapping, packaging, and cards, which wastes—you guessed it—trees. This doesn't mean you should be stingy with your generosity; it just means you should be giving green.

How to Do It

One way to give green is to simply buy a charity gift card for your friend or relative. You buy the card from an organization like JustGive.org or CharityNavigator.org, and the recipient simply goes online and chooses which charity gets that gift—no packaging or waste, and it's for a good cause! You can also give money to an eco-charity in the name of a friend at changingthepresent.org. Traditional gift certificates and cards also make great green gifts because they don't have to be wrapped or

packaged. And they give your friends the opportunity to buy whatever they like. That means no more fake "Thank you—I love it!" smiles, or tossing of unwanted crap. Other green gifts include treating a friend to a movie, concert, or dinner out. These types of gifts come with zero packaging or need for returns, and they give you an opportunity to spend time with the friend you are treating, which is always the most memorable gift of all (no, really, it is).

When you do buy actual presents, try and purchase things that are biodegradable, like plants or food (who wouldn't love gourmet chocolate or a subscription to the Hot Sauce of the Month Club?), or things that are easily re-giftable, such as books and music.

While You're At It

If you do buy a present that can be wrapped, resist the wrapping. Gift packaging isn't just wasteful, it's expensive. Instead of wrapping a present in colorful paper or putting it in a shiny bag filled with ribbon, use the Sunday comics, a reusable shopping bag, your last book report, or pages from last year's phonebook. Or use the Japanese tradition of wrapping your present in cloth (like a scarf) that the recipient can use, making the wrapping part of the present.

28 Keep It Local

Like drinking yerba maté tea from Paraguay? Or eating chocolates from Belgium? People have always loved stuff that comes from far away: silks from China, kiwifruit from New Zealand, coffee from Costa Rica. But products from far away come with a problem: a lot of fuel is needed to get them here. So, conscious consumers are starting to buy more local things. That's good for the environment because it means less of the air pollution that stems from the burning fuel of the transporting plane, train, or truck. It also makes us more independent as a country because the less fuel we need, the less we need to depend on other countries to get it to us.

There are other good reasons to buy local. Because locally grown produce hasn't traveled far and wide, it's often fresher (often just picked), filled with more nutrients, and tastes better than something that's been sitting on a supermarket shelf for three days or truck bed for two weeks. When you buy locally grown foods, you also keep money within the community, making for a healthier local economy.

And even if you subsist daily on peanut butter sandwiches and chocolate bars (which is kind of gross, but whatever), there are lots of things besides groceries that you can get from local producers. Clothing designers, toymakers, beauty product inventors, pet food suppliers, artists, and all sorts of people are likely producing and selling their own stuff right in your neighborhood. You just have to be on the lookout for it.

How to Do It

Start by going to a farmers' market. These markets are generally held outdoors and happen year-round across the country; they offer the very best of every season's produce, plus tons of other goodies like fresh cookies and cakes, warm apple cider, funky arts and crafts, and sometimes even CDs from local bands. Go to localharvest.org or foodroutes.org for more info and to find a market near you.

You can shop locally for other kinds of products, too. Head to the neighborhood ice cream parlor that's owned by your friend's mom; print your photos at a local lab that prints in-house (instead of shipping your order to another location many miles away); buy CDs of local bands and art by local artists; and buy clothing from hometown designers instead of shops at the mall (you'll have the added bonus of wearing something unique that not everyone else at school owns!).

29 Go Organic

Y ou've heard about the recent organic craze, but what exactly is "organic"? Organic produce is produce that's grown with minimal pesticides, synthetic fertilizers, or hormones. Organic meat and milk come from animals that are not treated with antibiotics or hormones. It's easy to see that organic foods are simply more natural. But what you may not have known is that they're also better for the environment. Since they're grown with almost no synthetic pesticides, it's less likely that dangerous chemicals will leak into the soil or water systems. In fact, studies have found that some organic farming methods actually improve soil by increasing its number of beneficial organisms and nutrients.

So how do you know if food is organic? You have to read labels. But just because something says "natural" or "pesticide-free" doesn't mean it is organic. Look for the sticker that says "USDA Organic," which means the product has been certified by the United States Department of Agriculture to have at least 95 percent organic ingredients, excluding water and salt.

How to Do It

One thing you might notice as you start filling your basket with organic foods: the price tags. Because organic foods sometimes take longer to produce—farmers often rotate, till, and mulch crops to limit weeds instead of simply spraying chemical herbicides—they tend to cost more. Here are a few guide-lines for getting the most bang out of your organic buck.

- Buy in-season, when more farmers are producing the same kinds of crops and pricing is more competitive.

- Comparison shop at farmers' markets (also see page 67), where many organic farmers may be selling goods at the same time.

- See if your local supermarket has a discounted organic food line. (But be sure the products are locally grown!)

Don't Stop at Food

You can also go organic with flowers and clothes. Many flowers sold in the United States are grown with pesticides. As an alternative, buy naturally grown organic flowers from local farmers. Also, opt for clothing that consists of 100 percent organic cotton (see page 62), which has been grown and harvested without pesticides.

30 Tune It Up

So you finally got a car? Great—**greenify** it! The first step is to get a tune-up. Unless it's really obvious that your car is in need of its yearly check-up—like it's puttering so slowly down the street that little old ladies are passing you left and right with their walkers—you may forget to take it to the mechanic. But don't. Regular car maintenance will leave you with better fuel economy (how many miles you can go per gallon), which reaps these benefits:

- You save precious **fossil fuels** from being used to make gasoline.

- You curb the emission of **carbon dioxide** into the atmosphere (1 gallon of gasoline produces 20 pounds of carbon dioxide when burned, so the fewer gallons you burn, the cleaner you leave the air.).

- You shell out less cash at the gas station (yes!).

An annual engine tune-up can improve your gas mileage by as much as 4 percent. And when you get a tune-up, you can also replace clogged air filters and add air to your tires, both of which improve your gas mileage even more.

How to Do It

To schedule a tune-up, simply call your mechanic and make an appointment. To see what effect the tune-up has from year to year on your car, check your fuel economy (how much gas you are using per mile) before and after the tune-up.

To check your fuel economy (aka miles per gallon), do this:

1. Fill your tank.

2. Reset your odometer to zero.

3. The next time you get gas, write down the mileage that appears on the odometer.

4. Divide that number by how many gallons it took to fill the tank—that number is your "miles per gallon."

The higher the number, the better. It should go up if you are getting regular tune-ups. If it seems to be going down, talk to a mechanic to see what you can do about it. (When doing this experiment, be sure to drive your car on the same types of roads—such as city roads or freeways— before and after you reset the odometer, as your speed and the amount of breaking and accelerating you do also affects your mileage.)

CALCULATE It!

If you want to learn more about the fuel economy of your particular car, go to fueleconomy.gov, click on the Find a Car tab, and then search for your car. You'll find out how many tons of greenhouse gas emissions your car is responsible for, about how much money you're spending on gas, and your air pollution score.

31 Turn It Off

How many times have you (or your friends) kept the car's engine running in the driveway so that you could hear the end of your favorite song, make a quick call on your cell phone, or warm it up on a cold, wintry morning?

Yep, guilty as charged. You only do it for a few minutes at a time, of course, but multiply that by the millions of other drivers who do it, too, and you'll see that it adds up fast. The US Environmental Protection Agency estimates that a car puts approximately 6.6 grams of pollutants (including nitrous oxide) into the air for every minute it sits and idles.

If you are going to be stopping somewhere for more than 30 seconds, turning the car off will also save you gas. As for letting the car engine warm up on a cold day, experts say it's unnecessary. Modern vehicles need little warm-up, and idling for long periods in cold weather can actually cause excessive engine wear.

How to Do It

Turn off your engine when your car isn't moving (how's that for an uncomplicated answer?). And by the way, "isn't moving" means your car is still sitting in the driveway or standing at a curb, not stopped waiting for a red light to change (switching off the engine of a standard gas vehicle while it's stopped in traffic is dangerous). If you want to hear a song play out, or look at something with the interior light, just turn the key partially so that the engine is off but the battery is still on. Caution: Do not do this for long stretches of time or your battery will die and you'll need someone to come jump start your car. Playing the radio for 5 minutes while the engine is off, though, shouldn't present a problem.

Let the Pros Wash It

It's true: It's better to let the pros wash your car than to do it yourself. For one, when you wash at home, the icky water doused in toxic car muck trickles into the storm drains and then eventually into our waterways where it poisons aquatic life. At car washes, they drain wastewater into sewer systems, so it gets treated before it is discharged back into the great outdoors. Plus, the computer-controlled systems and high-pressure pumps that the pros use help minimize water usage. The average car wash at home uses 80-140 gallons of water, while the average commercial car wash only uses 45 gallons. Some places even recycle and reuse their rinse water!

32 Jump in the Pool

The next time you're in a car and waiting for the light to turn green, look at the car next to you, the one in front of you, and the one behind you. What do you notice? Odds are, each car is carrying just one person: the driver.

More cars are out cruising the highways now than ever before, which adds up to lots of traffic and major air pollution. Cars produce **hydrocarbons**, nitrogen oxides, and **carbon monoxide**, which are all ingredients of **smog**. If you get to school (or wherever) via car, traveling with even just one friend goes a long way in eliminating environmental toxins and saving fuel sources. And here's an added incentive for longer trips: Packing in three or more people also qualifies your vehicle to travel in the carpool lanes on the highway, which usually go way faster than the other lanes. In some cities, carpooling even gets you free access over bridges during commute hours.

How to Do It

The best way to start? Mention the idea to friends who live near you, neighbors, and people at school. Ask people who have schedules that are similar to yours. Send out a message on Facebook that you're looking to carpool.

Once you find people who want to share a ride, it's organization time. Determine your route, come up with a schedule, and decide who drives when. Ask your parents to take part if you're not yet driving—or legally allowed to drive other minors around. Then, talk about money. This can be a sticky point of business if not everyone in the carpool shares equal driving responsibilities, but it's important to determine what's fair right away. As a general rule, everyone should equally split gas (and tolls, if there are any). People who don't ever drive might consider throwing in a few extra dollars since the driver (or the driver's parent) is the one who also has to maintain the car, and pay for car insurance.

Reduce Your Need for Speed

Drive faster, get there faster, use less gas. Right? Wrong. Speeding wastes gas. In fact, it can lower your gas mileage (or fuel economy, see page 71) by 33 percent when you are driving on the highway. And it can hurt your wallet: Each 5 mph you drive over 60 mph is like paying an additional $0.24 per gallon for gas! Slow down to help save money *and* the planet.

33 Go on an Eco-Adventure

I f you live in a city—or even a suburb—you might find that your opportunities to commune with nature are often limited to a picnic in a bustling park, with squirrels trying to steal your lunch. Without exposure to the oceans, mountains, and forests of the world, it's hard to grow a true appreciation for them, and become committed to protecting them. If you never leave the city, or if you only leave it to go to over-crowded beach resorts where people are accidentally harming delicate ecosystems and leaving behind litter and pollution—it's time to get out there and get to know your planet the responsible way.

Taking an eco-adventure can be as simple as taking an environmentally conscious camping trip with your family. But you can also sign up for a more structured trip that specifically teaches you to better understand and appreciate the environment. These trips, sometimes called eco-tours, involve learning how to white-water raft, bike, hike, scuba dive, or kayak while also learning about the biodiversity of the region—what makes it special, what dangers it faces, and the things that you can do to help save it—through an environmentally conscious local guide. Some trips are more about self-empowerment, perhaps felt from navigating rough waters by canoe, and others are aimed at working on specific tasks within a community, like counting baby turtles during hatching season or helping to measure coral reefs. In the end, you meet a lot of cool people, gain a better understanding of a particular region, and develop a whole new respect for the environment. When was the last time a trip to Disney World did all that?

How to Do It

Eco-tourism can be pricey, especially for a teen, so it's best to search for organizations that offer special prices and trips to students. Three great programs that offer student fellowships and scholarships to teens are Earthwatch Institute (earthwatch.org), Outward Bound (outwardbound.org), and National Outdoor Leadership School (nols. edu). Earthwatch offers programs around the world in which you can help protect endangered black sea turtles in Baja, monitor climate change in the Arctic, or observe macaws of the Peruvian Amazon all while learning a new language and meeting other (potentially cute) people your age. Outward Bound and National Outdoor Leadership School offer expert-led US adventures in the great outdoors, in which you also learn leadership skills. Make sure to do plenty of research before proposing the idea to your parents so you are prepared to answer their questions.

34 Be a Green Guest

When people take a vacation, they often take a vacation from responsibility, too. That's not entirely a bad thing. How else would anyone get into the mindset of paragliding or bungee-jumping? But taking a break from the day-to-day responsibilities of homework and part-time jobs doesn't mean stomping all over the poor planet.

Our behavior at hotels is one of the biggest problems. We have our linens washed daily for us, and are provided with an endless stream of hot water—what's not to love about that? But all of this luxury equals serious consequences for the environment. More and more hotels are becoming eco-friendly, offering programs and facilities that conserve water and energy. You've seen the signs posted in hotel bathrooms asking you to reuse your towels as often as you can, haven't you? That's a good start, but there is a lot more you can do to help cut down the amount of waste generated wherever you stay—a hotel, motel, or B&B.

How to Do It

- **Just say "no" to hotel shampoos.** In America alone, there are about 50,000 hotels. Now think if hotel management leaves out two small bottles for each hotel room every day. That's an enormous amount of little plastic bottles that may not even get recycled. And what about all of that shampoo that goes to waste when you don't finish the bottle? The answer is to bring your own toiletries. That doesn't mean buying "travel toiletries" as that's also a waste of plastic—and money. (Travel items cost way more per ounce than regular-size ones.) Instead, pour your own products from home into reusable plastic containers that are the right size for your trip.

- **Don't have your sheets or towels washed every day.** Sure, it's a luxury to have clean linens and towels every day, but that's all it is. Washing a set of bed sheets and a pair of bathroom towels requires about 12-16 gallons of water. Now multiply that by each hotel guest who gets barely touched linens and once-used towels washed each day. It equals a mega water waste. See if there is a policy for requesting that your towels and linens get washed weekly (or not all, if you're only there for a short stay). In some hotels, it's as simple as hanging towels back up on a hook. In others, you may need to call the front desk and make a personal request.

- **Turn off the lights.** You do it when you're at home, right? Do it at the hotel, too. Studies have shown that, in hotels, the majority of energy expended through lighting comes from the bathroom light being left on for more than one hour! After you're done with your business, remember to hit the switch!

These tips are also useful for trips to a friend's or relative's house—they will not only save plastic, water, and electricity, but also save your hosts a lot of money.

35 Have a "Stuff" Sale

Spring cleaning is so awesome. You get to clear your room out of all of those eighth-grade posters, fifth-grade lunchboxes, and, depending on whether you've ever done spring cleaning before, maybe even your first grade Barbies and Barneys. But what should you do with all of it? You don't want to just throw perfectly usable stuff away and add more to landfills. So why not host a garage, yard, or street sale? It's a great way to get rid of a lot of stuff, hang out with friends, make some money, and give the local sanitation workers a break.

How to Do It

1. **Snare some cohorts.** It is way easier and a lot more fun to do a "stuff" sale with friends.

2. **Pick a day for the sale.** And make sure it's OK with your parents. Chances are they'll even want to help you—or at least give you stuff to sell.

3. **Get clearance.** Find out if you need permission from the city or your community to host a sale.

4. **Advertise.** Make a website about it and send out a link, post it on Facebook, pass out fliers at the grocery store, take out an ad in the paper, and post signs *everywhere*. (There might be city or community rules about where you can post fliers, so be sure to ask.)

5. **Collect the goods.** Pull together the toys that have been shoved in the closet for the last decade, the old books, and the kiddie games. You may be tempted to grab your dad's old plaid shorts or your mom's embarrassing 1980s T-shirts, but try and focus on your own stuff first.

6. **Price it.** A good rule of thumb is to mark things that are in good condition at one-quarter or one-third the price they would have sold for new. But look at your stuff objectively: Just because you paid $120 for that shaggy orange-and-green coat doesn't mean anyone will think it's worth $40.

7. **Arrange it.** Lay things out so they're easy for customers to see (and so your stuff looks as desirable as possible). If you're selling an old toy, sweep off the pile of dust. If you're selling any clothing, make sure it's clean before putting it out to sell.

8. **Sell it.** Make sure there is a cash box, plenty of singles and change, and someone available to take money at all times. And put up a sign that says "All sales final" so someone doesn't come back the next day when they've changed their mind about that Britney Spears CD.

36 Swap, Don't Shop!

You keep hearing about recycling, right? But it doesn't end with bottles, cans, and paper. Clothing takes a huge amount of natural resources to make (see page 60), and buying loads of new clothing (or throwing out old clothing) is not healthy for the environment. So what to do with all those perfectly-good-but-you're-maybe-a-little-sick-of-them clothes piled on your bedroom floor? Hold a clothing swap! It's the ideal way to get rid of your castoffs, score clothes from your friends, and have a party all at the same time.

How to Do It

A successful swap depends on the selection of clothes, the organization of the event, and, obviously, how much fun is had. It's really easy to do. Here are a few pointers.

1. Invite 5–10 people so you have a nice selection. (Less people than that, and there may not be enough things to choose from; more than that, and it turns into a feeding frenzy.)

2. Tell everyone to bring clean clothes in good condition, plus plenty of reusable bags to tote their "new" clothes home.

3. Put out some snacks.

4. Assign different surfaces in the room (the floor, a table, a sofa, a bed) a different type of clothing (tops, pants, skirts, accessories). Have everyone put their clothes in the right spots.

5. Place a few mirrors around your room so people can see how things look when they try them on. (One of the ground rules of the swap should be that everyone must try on an item before they claim it—things always look different when you put them on.)

6. Try to have at least one bathroom and/or closet available for those who are a little more modest.

7. Establish a starting time. Maybe you say "go," or turn on a certain song, or whatever. Just keep music playing throughout—remember, it's a party!

8. If two people are doing a tug-of-war over the same pair of jeans, have them toss a coin to decide who gets it. Keep it light!

9. Donate whatever clothes are left over to a charity or shelter, or sell them at your "stuff" sale (see page 80).

37 Host a Green Film Festival

ometimes it takes a little creativity to get people to care about our planet. *National Geographic* magazine might make you want to jump up and do cartwheels, but to your friends, it might be a snooze. But just about everyone is into movies. So break out the popcorn (organic, of course) and invite a bunch of friends over to watch flicks about the environment. From action and adventure to indie to blockbuster, there are a kajillion movies (give or take) in which the environment plays a starring role.

How to Do It

It's easy to host a great **green** film festival. Here are some tips.

1. **Pick a venue.** For a small festival (say 5 to 10 friends), hold it at your house. For a larger group (say, a whole soccer team or cheer squad), ask your school if you can borrow a room, a screen, and DVD player.

2. **Pick a time.** If the film festival is at your place, you can make it a Friday or Saturday night affair that can go from 7 pm until as late as your parents allow. If it's at school, it's probably better to do it on a Saturday or Sunday afternoon. Film festivals are all different lengths, depending on how many movies are shown. If you have a full 6 hours, you can easily show three movies in a row. But if you know your audience is a little attention deficient, keep it down to 1 or 2 hours and then continue the festival the next

day or weekend. Either way, keep it separate from your school schedule so people will see it as a party and not an assignment.

3. **Choose your films.** You have to be something of a curator when organizing a film festival. Select your films based on how relevant they are to the message you are trying to share, and, even if you show only two movies, make it a good combination of both serious and cute/funny so that the films appeal to everyone, and they all have a good time.

Green Film Festival Picks

Gorillas in the Mist: The Story of Dian Fossey (1988), *Baraka* (1992), *FernGully: The Last Rainforest* (1992), *Erin Brockovich* (2000), *The Day After Tomorrow* (2004), *An Inconvenient Truth* (2006), *The Simpsons Movie* (2007), *Food, Inc* (2009), *Avatar* (2010).

4. **Collect donations.** Choose a reputable environmental organization that you'd like to support and ask attendees to bring a few bucks to donate. Be prepared to give people solid info about where their money is going.

5. **Get eco-food.** Make sure you supply organic (see page 68) and local (see page 66) treats that come in a minimal amount of packaging.

38 Go on a Green Date

oing on an environmentally friendly date doesn't have to be geeky or gross. You don't have to spend your afternoon picking up rusty old cans and squished bottles from that park downtown—unless that's your way of wooing. A green date is really about making more careful decisions when you plan. Take a moment to think about what you do on a regular date. You probably start by taking a car (uh-oh—air pollution and fossil fuel use) to order something to eat that you won't finish (hmmm … food waste?), and then hop back in the car (more air pollution and fossil fuel) to go to a movie (where your popcorn box and candy wrappers will add to piles of trash). At least the goodnight kiss is totally eco-friendly! (That is, unless you are making out while the car is idling (see page 72). Don't fret! The most romantic things in life are the most eco-friendly. With a little thought, it's easy to dream up a great date that will leave you feeling giddy and green.

How to Do It

Try these suggestions:

- **Go on a picnic.** Pack homemade food into reusable, environmentally friendly containers. Take along real plates and silverware, and walk or ride your bikes to the nearest park.

- **Do something ed-date-cational.** Hit up the latest exhibit at the natural history museum, visit the botanical gardens, or check out the zoo.

Educational rendezvous are so much better in a date setting than on a school trip. Use public transportation to get there, too!

- **Rent a movie.** Watch movies at home, which uses fewer natural resources than at the theater and provides a fun excuse to cuddle. Pick an environmental film (see page 85), and bake your own cookies (using organic eggs and milk—see page 68) as snacks.

- **Go stargazing.** Go to a quiet and safe spot on a clear night and marvel at the millions of stars (and the occasional meteorite) while stealing eco-friendly kisses in the dark.

39 Order the Green Plate Special

So, you're out to dinner with your friends and everyone is finished eating, sitting around chatting and laughing—amid piles and piles of uneaten food. You're not alone. Americans throw away more than 34 million tons of food waste each year. On average, that ends up being about 219 pounds of food thrown away by each person. That's like throwing out a whole person (or two!).

While a lot of the tossed food comes from our homes (milk goes sour, bread goes moldy), some of it also comes from restaurants. Many of the more than 900,000 restaurants in the United States dole out portions that are more than twice the size of a nutritionist's suggested portion. We can't eat everything on our plates because our plates are enormous … so we leave food there and it goes straight to the dump, where it produces the greenhouse gas methane. Ick.

This doesn't mean you should eat until you're sick to avoid adding to landfills. It just means you should think a little before you order.

How to Do It

Simply order less. Ask your server if half-portion sizes are available, or order an appetizer as your main entrée, since those are often smaller. You could even split a dish with your dinner partner, which conserves food and saves money (note that some restaurants have "sharing fees" when you do this). It's best to start off small, and order more food if you are still hungry later.

Taking It To Go

The great news about doggie bags is that they mean less food wasted. The downside is all the packaging. When you ask for a to-go bag, request that the restaurant use as few packaging items as possible—for example, take the carton of leftover General Tso's chicken, but not paper napkins, plastic utensils, or a plastic bag to carry it in. (You get extra points for you if you bring your own container!)

There's always a reason to celebrate: birthdays, graduations, holidays, acing your driving test, the end of the semester, the beginning of summer, the DVD release of your favorite film. And as anyone who has ever thrown a party knows, the biggest post-party bummer (apart from the possibility of being grounded) is the sheer volume of waste. Crumpled paper napkins, crushed cans, half-eaten bags of chips, plastic cups broken into sad little shards on the floor—and that's just after one party. Imagine the mess left from all the parties that rage all around the world. Where does all of this trash go? To the landfills, of course. So, when throwing a party, it's important to minimize waste.

How to Do It

You don't have to stand around eating organic apples at the community garden (see page 98) to have an eco-friendly shindig. You just have to make some minor changes. Here are a few suggestions.

- **Send e-invitations instead of paper ones.** OK, you probably do this anyway—it's quick, it's easy, and it's less clumsy than retro paper invites. But it's also the most environmentally sound choice. If there are any wannabe Martha Stewarts in your crowd who say it's tacky to use e-cards, tell them it's tackier to pollute water by using traditional stationary, which is typically bleached with chlorine at paper mills in a process that releases toxins that don't break down in water and hurt fish and birds. That should keep them quiet.

- **Allow each person only one cup.** You know how easy it is to lose your drink when everyone else has identical ones? You put it down for a second, realize you don't know which cup belongs to you, then reach for a brand-new one. The result: A lot of cups are tossed for no reason. Try a new system of handing each guest a cup that you mark with their name. Or hand the duty over to your circle's best artist, who can craft funny caricatures or artsy monograms to ensure no one will let their cup go astray.

- **Streamline the garbage.** Reduce waste by buying party foods in bulk (less packaging to throw out) and send guests home with leftover snacks. Instead of handing out disposable paper plates for people's pizza, use plates you can wash and reuse. If your mom's ceramic or porcelain dishes are not available, durable plastic ones can be used over and over again for your and your friends' parties. And, most important, make it easy for your guests to recycle. Put out two trash cans and label them clearly, making it obvious that one is for straight trash and the other is for cans, bottles, and other recyclable goods.

41 Get Greens for Greening

There are little things you can do to help the environment just throughout the course of a normal day, and then there are big things. But to do the big things, you need money, and that's where a grant comes in.

A grant is basically a gift of money from a person, organization, or government agency that goes directly to your cause. Winning a grant can make all the difference in achieving your get-green goal. In the past, teens have won grants that helped them do everything from launching recycling programs to helping raise money to provide clean drinking water to students in Africa.

How to Do It

We all have an environmental cause we're passionate about. With yours in mind, come up with a concrete goal you'd like to achieve. ("To get a group of people together to remove garbage from the northeast section of the river and its banks" is good, whereas simply "To clean up the river" is more ambiguous and less likely to motivate you to get it done, or convince a grant board that you've got a clear objective.)

Once you set your goal, find an organization that supports your cause, and see what kinds of grants they offer. Read the guidelines carefully. If you don't see a grant that fits your cause, your age, and your needs, call the organization to find out if they have other grants or if they are willing to let you propose a totally new one.

Your grant proposal has to be stellar. Some grants require lengthy applications and recommendations from teachers; others even ask for detailed essays and videos. Be as specific as possible when talking about your cause, what you would use the money for, and what goals you expect to achieve. Note the due dates of applications, then leave yourself enough time to revise, edit, and polish your application until it's so perfect, they couldn't *not* give it to you.

Check out the Green Resources section on (page 112) to find specific places that offer grants.

42 Turn Free Time Into Green Time

What do eating chocolate, exercising, and volunteering all have in common? Each activity triggers the release of endorphins—feel-good hormones that help eliminate stress. But only one of the three has the potential to help the environment, too: volunteering. Donating your time to the environment not only feels good, but it puts you in touch with like-minded people. And it doesn't even have to disrupt your schedule all that much. Even one day a week can make a difference.

How to Do It

Environmental organizations and clubs need volunteers to help with just about everything, so there's a good chance you can contribute in a meaningful way that's also fun for you. You could participate in go-green legislative and educational campaigns to increase awareness about global warming, raise funds to protect domestic and wild animals, keep park trails tidy and litter-free, or make a website for a local environmental charity with limited resources.

When deciding what kind of environmental volunteering position is best for you, ask yourself these questions:

- What causes are you most passionate about?

- How much time can you spare (one day a week, one day a month)? Remember that cramming in too much may exhaust you and shortchange your current responsibilities—plus you could end up leaving the organization you originally wanted to help shorthanded.

- Do you want to do something hands-on, such as take care of a community garden (see page 98), or go behind-the-scenes to assist with administrative tasks, like filing papers or writing grants.

If you don't have any specific organization in mind, check out volunteermatch.org to find eco-organizations near you or contact any of the organizations in our Green Resources section (see page 112) to see if they need help. Find an organization you like? Talk with current volunteers to see what sorts of projects you'd be doing and how they like the work.

Get a Green Internship

Internships are basically sophisticated volunteer postions in which you trade your time in exchange for job experience. They are often more demanding than regular volunteer positions, but they'll give you a better taste of what it is like to have an environmental job. Green internships are great additions to college applications. See the organizations in our Green Resources section (see page 112) for ideas on places to contact. The environmental social network Planet Connect, for example, (planetconnect.org) devotes a whole section of its site to internship possibilities.

43 Yours Treely

Environmentalists often get tagged as "tree-huggers," and for good reason: We love trees! Why? Trees absorb carbon dioxide from our environment, which is important because too much carbon dioxide in the atmosphere directly contributes to the greenhouse effect. In one year, a mature tree can absorb up to 48 pounds of carbon dioxide from the atmosphere, and give off enough oxygen to support two people. A mature tree also absorbs other pollutants like smog-causing ozone and carbon monoxide. And the leafy branches of trees provide shade, which cuts down on energy costs in summer. Knowing all of this, who wouldn't want to hug a tree? And what better tree to hug than the one you plant yourself?

How to Do It

Tree-planting is a great way for people in the community to come together and celebrate the earth. You can even dedicate the tree to someone special, like a friend, an environmental advocate, or a loved one. Below are some different approaches you can take.

1. **Donate a tree.** If you don't want to muck around with mulch, you can pledge funds to a nonprofit organization, like Trees for the Future (plant-trees.org), which will plant the tree for you. This is the no muss, no fuss option; the organization will research what tree works best with what climate and plant it for you.

2. **Help another group.** Work with your school, city, or local environmental group to raise funds to purchase a tree and plant it in a prominent place.

3. **Plant it yourself, in your community, or at school.** To do this, you'll need to gather a team of planters and then get permission from the city council or the school administration. You'll need to raise money to buy the tree and everything that goes with it: tree delivery, tools, and possibly even fees for experts who will take over the tree-selection process and actual planting. (Call a local nursery to find experts and organizations that can help you.) After that, your team will need to find the right tree for the right place (planting a tree won't do much good if you live in the desert but end up choosing a tree that thrives only in rainy climates). The fun part is planting day, when you invite everyone from the neighborhood or school to watch the new tree take root.

Getting Started

Planting a tree is a big undertaking. Here are some sites that can help get you started.

- TreePeople (treepeople.org)
- Arbor Day Foundation (arborday.org)
- Tree Musketeers (treemusketeers.org)
- Trees for the Future (plant-trees.org)

44 Get Growing

If you think carrots and tomatoes grow on supermarket shelves, it might be time to branch out and start your own community garden. Growing your own food may sound complicated, and it does take some energy to get it going, but it's also a lot of fun.

So what is a community garden? Basically, it's a collaborative project in which a group of people transform an area of land—an overgrown or neglected lot, for instance—into a living, breathing entity. It can be urban, suburban, or rural, and produce all different types of flowers, fresh fruits, veggies, and herbs. A community garden is *great* for the environment. It makes use of sometimes otherwise wasted land, cultivates it with rich, vitamin-filled soil, and adds nourishing (and pretty!) plants. And those fresh-grown fruits and veggies don't have to travel anywhere by boat, truck, or plane (no fossil fuels used) before they get to your table.

How to Do It

First, form a group of people to work with. Outline the responsibilities for everyone, which will include attending meetings, planting and caring for your plants, and keeping the garden well maintained. Make sure there is at least one good gardener in your group.

Next, go on a mission to find a piece of land. It should be vacant, get about 8 hours of sunlight a day, have an H_2O hookup, and be centrally located in the community, making it easy for all your gardeners and visitors to get to. A great option is an open plot of land at a school in your area. If you find one, present your garden idea to the school administrators. If you want to use a spot that's privately owned, you will need permission from the owner. Find out who the owner is, and then approach him or her with your idea. Explain what a community garden is, and how he or she will benefit from the garden (their neglected property will be beautified and taken care of for free!). If they agree, get your parents to help draw up a lease, which can be for as little as $1 a year.

Then, come up with a plan. Will everyone tend to all the plants, or will people have their own individual plots? How will you split the costs of supplies? With the help of the group, design your space and choose what to grow (read up on this first!). Confer with your gardener friend and get together all the things you'll need, including tools, lumber, watch sources, and sunscreen.

Need Help?

See if there are any community groups that can lend resources and expertise. Call city parks and park superintendents to see if they can offer money, labor, or even just advice. Check out communitygarden.org for more pointers.

Bin There, Do That

By now, you know the drill: recycle. But what happens when you live in an area that's not exactly recycling-friendly? Do you notice that when you go to your mom's office, tons of paper gets thrown out with the regular trash? Or that the garbage can at your school is always filled with soda bottles and cans? Believe it or not, you can do something about it. Whether it's for your neighborhood, your city, your school, or your parent's workplace, you can help decrease huge mountains of waste by starting a recycling program.

How to Do It

Decide where you want to start your recycling program and propose the idea to a point person who can help you make it happen—maybe your principal, your mom's boss, or the president of your neighborhood association. When proposing your idea, be specific about what kinds of waste you notice occurring, and what kind of program you think is necessary to address the situation. That point person may offer to take matters into his or her own hands—which would be great. If so, suggest that he or she research what kinds of trash the establishment puts out and find a recyclables vendor to work with, or simply enforce an already existing recycling plan that no one uses.

You may also be asked to come up with a plan of your own. What plan you create depends on certain things. If it is public property, you'll need to petition the city council or another arm of the city government (check your city's website) to see if it's in the town's or city's ability to administer the program. If it's private, you may need to raise funds to pay for recycling bins and for someone to come take away all the paper, plastic, and glass you collect. Often an area is already recycling-friendly (pickup service and bins are available), and you just need to put a few bins out and teach people how to recycle.

Whatever form the plans for recycling take, get the word out! Distribute handouts, make announcements, talk to people personally. Remember that the more people who are aware and reminded, the more likely they are to put your plan into action. For more pointers, check out earth911.com/how-to/how-to-start-a-recycling-program.

46 Get Political

Think politics is just a bunch of people talking about boring stuff that doesn't have anything to do with you? You might be surprised that politicians are actually talking about and debating topics that will directly affect how you live—topics such as the environment and **global warming**. Interesting, important stuff. And you don't have to be older (or even old enough to vote) to get involved with politics. In fact, politicians often don't get to hear from teenagers about what issues are important to them. But you can change that.

How to Do It

More and more candidates have **green** platforms, meaning the environment is near the top of their priority lists. Whenever there is an election, read up on the candidates and see who is greenest. Watch them debate and look at where they stand on environmental issues. If you find a candidate who has good ideas, show your support by helping out his or her campaign. Check out the candidate's website for ways to get involved. Even if you're not yet 18 and can't vote, there are lots of other things you can do to help—like making calls, handing out fliers, and stuffing envelopes. A lot of politicians actually got their start in politics when they were teens, so who knows, this could be the beginning of a career in public policy for you!

When it's not election time, there are other ways to support green issues. The main one is by using your voice. See the Green Resources page on page 112 for more organizations with which you can get involved. Write a letter to your local newspaper or an article for your school newspaper about green issues and policies that you think need to be changed. Or join a larger online teen activism community—such as TeenActivist.org or MTV Act (act.mtv.com)—where you can post videos, opinions, and bring other teens' (and adults') attention to issues that matter.

47 Spread the Word

Y ou know a lot about the environment now—what's hurting it and how to help it. But keeping all that information to yourself is just as dangerous as not knowing it in the first place. The only way to truly help the planet is to start making changes to your lifestyle while encouraging other people to do the same.

If the idea of telling everyone about the environment (and how to help it) brings on visions of you standing alone in the middle of a crowd and screeching into a megaphone, don't worry. You don't have to get on a high-and-mighty soapbox to preach what you practice.

How to Do It

- **Talk about it.** When you're out and about, let informational nuggets about the environment drop into conversation with your friends and family—and then move on. The last thing you want to do is irritate people with constant proselytizing. But if the subject of the planet comes up naturally, talk about the small things you do to help and then let your friends ask questions.

- **Write a blog.** Use any of the free blogging platforms already out there, like WordPress, Tumblr, or Blogger. If you already have a blog, make a discussion about eco-friendly living part of it. For instance, put in a "green tip of the day." Even if your audience is small—say, your best friend and your brother—that's still two people who will remember to bring a canvas shopping bag the next time they hit the grocery store.

- **Make a video.** Post a video on your YouTube or Vimeo to potentially reach millions of viewers. Of course, the key to nabbing some of those viewers lies in how you convey the message. When in doubt, opt for funny. For example, write a script that makes fun of the things we all do that hurt the environment—like maybe film someone throwing empty water bottles over his shoulder while lounging next to his SUV. It's OK for viewers to come away laughing, as long as they also get what your message is all about. You want people to forward the link to your masterpiece, and if it's both informative and amusing, you have a better chance of it getting sent around.

- **Take charge.** Are you disgusted by the amount of litter on your city's beaches or irritated with the increasing lack of local open green spaces? Organize a school effort to get the beaches clean or protest the razing of a local forest. Your efforts will pique the interest of newspapers and TV stations (really—the media love watching young people get involved with stuff like this), and help make people in your community think twice before throwing trash on the sand or driving their cars one block to the corner store.

Kermit the Frog once famously said, "It's not easy being green." But the truth is, once you're in the know, it's not as hard as it seems.

Glossary

aerobic: Living or occurring only in an environment with oxygen.

aluminum: A nonrenewable, metallic element that makes up about 7 percent of the earth's crust and takes energy to mine.

anaerobic: Living or occurring in an environment with no oxygen.

biodegradable: When something can decompose naturally. See also nonbiodegradable.

biodiversity: The number and variety of different organisms existing in a specific geographic area.

carbon dioxide (CO₂): A greenhouse gas that is emitted naturally when organic material decomposes, and unnaturally (as a pollutant by man) in large quantities when fuel from cars, buses, and planes is burned. Trees absorb CO₂, but when more of it is emitted into the atmosphere than trees can remove, it creates an imbalance that can cause global warming.

carbon monoxide (CO): An extremely poisonous gas that is emitted naturally through the carbon cycle, and unnaturally (as a pollutant by man) when oil, coal, and gas are burned. It can have serious health impacts on humans and animals.

chemical: A natural (water and salt) or man-made (dioxin and phthalates) substance with a defined molecular composition. Man-made chemicals can be toxic if not properly handled.

climate change: Short-term and long-term changes in our climate, such as changes in temperature patterns, precipitation and humidity levels, amount of sunlight and wind, etc. Climate change affects many aspects of earth life, from where and how people, plants, and animals live to food production, water use, and health risks. **Global warming** is a major cause of climate change.

compost: A mixture of soil and decaying garbage (including food) that helps fertilize and condition the earth. Composting puts organic, **biodegradable** matter back into the earth and keeps it out of **landfills**.

conserve: To protect **natural resources**.

crude oil: A dark oil made up of mostly **hydrocarbons**, otherwise known as unrefined **petroleum**.

decompose: When bacteria and fungi break down matter, changing its **chemical** makeup and physical appearance. Also known as rotting or decaying.

dump: See **landfill**.

eco-friendly: See **environmentally friendly**.

ecosystem: A system in which living things interact with each other and their surroundings.

energy: What is needed to power everything from our homes to our appliances to even our bodies. Most commonly defined as "the ability to do work." Some of its forms: chemical energy, electrical energy, heat (thermal) energy, light (radiant) energy, mechanical energy, and nuclear energy. Energy often uses a lot of **natural resources**.

environmentally friendly (aka **green** or **eco-friendly**): When something is done or produced with the purpose ful intent to cause little or no harm to the environment.

fossil fuel: Fuel made from nonrenewable resources—like coal, petroleum, and natural gas—that comes from the remains of extremely old, decomposed organic material.

global warming: An increase in the earth's atmospheric and oceanic temperatures, which is widely accepted as being due to the increased emissions of greenhouse gases. Global warming is also commonly regarded as a cause of climate change.

green: See environmentally friendly.

greenhouse gas: A gas (such as carbon dioxide, nitrous oxides, or methane) that traps the heat from the sun and warms the earth.

groundwater: Water found underground between soil particles and cracks in rocks that is used for drinking, recreation, and growing crops.

hazardous waste: Products that may pose a danger to humans and the environment when not disposed of properly.

herbicide: A chemical agent used on plant crops to kill or inhibit growth.

household hazardous waste: Household products, such as paints, pesticides, solvents, and certain types of batteries, that may pose a danger to humans and the environment when not disposed of properly.

hydrocarbon: An organic compound made of hydrogen and carbon that can be found in petroleum products, natural gas, and coals, and is an ingredient in smog. Hydrocarbons can sometimes be toxic.

landfill (aka dump): An area where non-hazardous solid waste (most of your garbage) is deposited, spread in layers, compacted, and covered. There are also chemical landfills that house hazardous waste. Landfills produce the greenhouse gas methane. They often leak methane into the air and, when not properly managed, toxic waste into ground-water or soil.

methane (CH₄): A greenhouse gas that is naturally emitted through marshlands, oceans, gas hydrates, and wildfires, and unnaturally emitted (as a pollutant by man) as a result of the anaerobic decomposition of organic compounds (which happens in landfills), as well as from farm livestock emissions, coal mining, and waste management. Methane traps heat and contributes to global warming. As a greenhouse gas, methane is 21 times more powerful than carbon dioxide.

natural resources: Any raw materials created by nature that have value in our economy. Examples: timber, fresh water, and mineral deposits.

nitrous oxides (N₂O): A group of powerful greenhouse gases that are naturally emitted from oceans and

vegetation, and unnaturally emitted (as a pollutant by man) when fuel burns at high temperatures (like in sewage treatment and car engines). Nitrous oxides contribute to global warming, hamper plant growth, and can bond with other pollutants to become toxic.

non-biodegradable: Unable to decompose into environmentally safe waste materials in a natural environment with bacteria. See also biodegradable.

non-renewable: A natural resource that cannot be replenished by nature, either because people are using it up faster than it can be replenished, or because it cannot be naturally restored or replenished at all. For this reason, these resources are in limited supply. Examples: oil and coal.

ozone (O₃): A greenhouse gas that naturally exists in the upper atmosphere (stratosphere), and is unnaturally emitted (as a **pollutant** by man) into the lower atmosphere (troposphere) when gasoline and fuels combust. It plays an important role in the stratosphere to protect us from the sun's ultraviolet rays. But, when it's in the troposphere, it is the main element of **smog**, and can contribute to **global warming**.

pesticide: any substance or mixture of substances used to repel or destroy unwanted pests, such as insects and weeds.

petroleum (aka **crude oil**): A yellow-to-black liquid that is usually found in underground reservoirs and is a **non-renewable** natural resource. It can be used in products like gasoline and **plastics**.

plastic: A non-metallic, **synthetic substance** made from petroleum that can be molded into various shapes.

pollutants: Contaminants that affect human health or harm the environment. When these are emitted into the air, it creates air pollution.

post-consumer recycled: When a whole product that has been used by a consumer (like a water bottle or sheet of loose-leaf paper) is made into something new.

pre-consumer recycled: When unused excess materials that are typically thrown away in factories (such as paper cuttings or scrap metal) are made into something new.

recyclable: When something can be recovered, reprocessed, and reused instead of thrown out.

recycling: The process of reusing a product (beyond its intended use) or taking **recyclable** materials like paper, aluminum, and glass, and converting them into new materials.

renewable: Term used to refer to **natural resources** that can be replenished naturally over time. Examples: wind, sunlight, rain, tides, and geothermal heat.

smog: Smog is a harmful mixture of fog and smoke, primarily formed when sunlight interacts with certain **pollutants** like tropospheric ozone, nitrogen oxides and carbon monoxide, which come from many manmade sources, like automobile exhaust, power plants, and toxic paint.

synthetic: Manmade (artificially made).

toxic: Harmful or poisonous.

wastewater: Used water—from a home, community, farm, or industry—that contains waste.

water system: A system that collects, treats, stores, and distributes drinkable, usable water from source to consumer.

waterway: A river, bay, stream, or other passageway for water.

Green Resources

Want more information about green life? Looking for a green grant? Want to find a green teen community? Here are some great places to start.

Alliance to Save Energy
www.ase.org
Organization that promotes energy efficiency worldwide to improve the economy, environment, and energy security. Has a Green Schools section.

American Forest & Paper Association
www.afandpa.org
Trade group with lots of great information on forestry and paper production/recycling.

Carbonfund.org
www.carbonfund.org
Organization that aims to reduce our carbon footprints. Offers ideas on reducing energy consumption and decreasing and offsetting carbon emissions. Includes carbon footprint calculators.

Cultural Survival
www.culturalsurvival.org/current-projects/global-response
Organization that develops and implements letter-writing (and other types of) campaigns for green initiatives. Focuses on education and has a special youth section.

Do Something Youth Grants $
www.dosomething.org
Contest that offers one $500 grant once a week to someone under the age of 25 who has an idea for a community action project.

Earth 911
www.earth911.com
One-stop shop for recycling information, green news, tips, and locations.

EarthEcho International
www.earthecho.org
Nonprofit ocean-saving youth organization that offers call-to-action programs for teens, such as the Water Planet Challenge. Founded by the grandchildren of famous legendary explorer Jacques Yves Cousteau.

EarthNews TV
www.earthnews.tv
TV channel with video reports and podcasts that spotlight communities, organizations, and people who are working to change the environment.

EarthTeam
www.earthteam.net
Environmental network for teens and youth leaders. Includes links to *The Green News* and The Green Screen, a news magazine and TV show respectively created by and for teens.

Earthwatch Institute
www.earthwatch.org
Organization that awards fellowships to high school and college students, allowing them to assist scientists around the world with fieldwork.

EcoEarth.Info
www.ecoearth.info
Environment portal and search engine with breaking news, blogs, and tons of environmental links.

EElinked Networks
eelinked.naaee.net
Great place to search for programs, grants, and environmental study abroad opportunities for teens.

Environmental Media Association
www.ema-online.org
Organization that uses the power of the entertainment industry to help inspire environmental change. Initiatives include planting school gardens with young celebrities, and creating opportunities for celebrities to speak out on sustainable lifestyles.

Environmental Protection Agency High School Site
www.epa.gov/highschool
While no longer updated, this teen portal of the government's EPA is a good database of statistics and scientific info. Great resource for writing papers.

Global Green USA
www.globalgreen.org
National environmental organization that is focused on fighting global climate change through programs such as the National Green Schools Initiative. Partnered with Brad Pitt to spearhead The Holy Cross Project, an initiative to rebuild a new, sustainable Ninth Ward in New Orleans.

Gloria Barron Prize for Young Heroes
www.barronprize.org
Annual contest that chooses 10 winners (all under 18) for work they do in their local communities and for their commitment to improving the planet. Each winner receives $2,500 that can go toward college or the project for which they won.

Go Green Initiative

www.gogreeninitiative.org

Environmental program that teaches students to be responsible caretakers for the planet by starting with their school campuses. Active in all 50 states and in 39 countries, the organization provides tools, training, and sometimes even funding to jumpstart environmental programs.

Humane Teen

www.humaneteen.org

Teen branch of the Humane Society of the United States, dedicated to helping and protecting animals, which goes hand in hand with helping the environment. Includes contests, animal-friendly product reviews, and news.

Idealist.org

www.idealist.org

Humanitarian social networking site on which you can create a profile, search for green jobs and internships, and meet like-minded people.

National Audubon Society

www.audubon.org

Organization that focuses on restoring natural ecosystems, focusing on birds, wildlife, and their habitats for the benefit of humanity and the earth's biological diversity.

National Environmental Education Foundation

www.neefusa.org

Funded by the government, NEEF offers grants and programs for teens and their teachers to advance environmental action.

National Outdoor Leadership School

www.nols.edu

Organization that offers environmentally focused short- and long-term courses in the wilderness. Offers special trips for teens, as well as college credit and financial aid.

Nicodemus Wilderness Project

www.wildernessproject.org

Organization that offers a program called Apprentice Ecologist Initiative, which helps teens engage in environmental stewardship projects worldwide, including beach, river, and mountain trash cleanups, wildlife habitat restoration, and native tree planting. Also offers three $850 scholarships a year for winning essays.

Outward Bound

www.outwardbound.org

Organization that teaches leadership and outdoors skills through expert-led adventures all over the country. Offers scholarships for teens.

P2D2: Prescription Pill and Drug Disposal Program
www.p2d2program.org
Provides communities with the best, safest methods of throwing away pills and other medications to reduce the misuse and abuse of pharmaceuticals, and make the quality of water and wildlife safer for future generations.

People for the Ethical Treatment of Animals
www.peta2.org
Organization that acts on the behalf of animals. The teen-focused PETA2 site offers calls to action, guides to living cruelty-free, vegetarian recipes, and more.

Planet Green
planetgreen.discovery.com
Website (and 24-hour TV channel) dedicated to helping people live mindfully.

Roots & Shoots
www.rootsandshoots.org
Guided by the principles and vision of primatologist and environmentalist Dr. Jane Goodall, this organization connects youth from around the globe who want to create a better world.

Sierra Club
www.sierraclub.org
Oldest and largest grassroots environmental organization in the US with more than a million members.

Sierra Student Coalition
www.ssc.org
The national student chapter of the Sierra Club. A broad network of high school and college students from around the country, working to protect the environment.

TeenActivist.org
www.teenactivist.org
Website dedicated to teens who want to effect change. Includes section on environment. Offers information about volunteer and internship opportunities for high school students.

Teens Turning Green
www.teensturninggreen.org
Coalition led by teens to educate and advocate environmentally and socially responsible choices.

Teens for Planet Earth
www.teens4planetearth.com
Part of the Wildlife Conservancy, this teen-centered social networking site includes news, volunteer opportunities, and a resouce library.

The Story of Stuff

www.storyofstuff.com

Founded by Annie Leonard, the author of the book *The Story of Stuff*, this website has free movies on topics like: where trash goes when we throw it "away"; how cosmetics are made; the environmental impact of plastic water bottles; and much more.

Act MTV

act.mtv.com

MTV blog that encourages and supports people who are working to make changes in the world.

Tree Hugger

www.treehugger.com

Site dedicated to making green life mainstream. Has green news, a green gift guide, blogs, a free iPhone app, and a radio show.

Trees for the Future

www.plant-trees.org

Organization that helps communities around the world plant trees. Check out the site's videos and take a tour of the organization's projects via its Google Earth global tour.

U.S. Department of Energy

www.energy.gov

Department of the government that has a mission to promote scientific and techno-logical innovation to advance the national, economic, and energy security of the United States.

US Energy Information Administration

www.eia.gov

Department of the government that collects, analyzes, and shares energy information to assist in the creation of good environmental laws and practices.

Vegetarian Teen

www.vegetarianteen.com

Website dedicated to teens who live the veggie life.

World Wildlife Fund

www.worldwildlife.org

Organization devoted to protecting wildlife. WWF also awards scholarships and grants to future environmental leaders.

Youth Venture

www.genv.net

Program that helps teens start their own organizations, giving professional assistance and seed funding (up to $1,000 per project) for teen-led social ventures, including those pertaining to the environment.

Source Notes

Introduction
- Union of Concerned Scientists, ucsusa.org/
- Smithsonian National Zoological Park, nationalzoo.si.edu/
- Philadelphia Water Department, phila.gov/water/
- "Ocean Pollution: It Starts With Us—And It Ends With Us," Avian Web, avianweb.com/plasticinouroceans.html

1. Get a Clean Shave
- Mrs. Green, "Response from BIC About Recycling Disposable Razor Blades, My Zero Waste (blog), May 27, 2009, myzerowaste.com/2009/05/response-from-bic-about-recycling-disposable-razor-blades/
- "Superfund for Students and Teachers," US Environmental Protection Agency (EPA), epa.gov/superfund/students/
- "Razor Saver," Sustainable Village, sustainablevillage.com/products/razor-saver
- "Waste Reduction in the Home," Pennsylvania Department of Environmental Protection, dep.state.pa.us/dep/deputate/airwaste/wm/recycle/facts/reduce.htm
- "Triple Razor," Preserve, preserveproducts.com/products/personalcare/triple-razor.html
- "Depilatory Poisoning," MedlinePlus, nlm.nih.gov/medlineplus/ency/article/002697.htm

2. Put the Spin Cycle on Pause
- California Energy Commission: Consumer Energy Center, consumerenergycenter.org/
- Adams, Mike, "Highly Toxic Chemicals Are Found in Laundry Detergents, Dryer Sheets, Deodorants, Perfumes, Soaps and Other Household Products," Natural News, May 17, 2004, naturalnews.com/001061.html
- "Key Characteristics of Laundry Detergent Ingredients," US EPA, epa.gov/dfe/pubs/laundry/techfact/keychar.htm
- Levi Strauss & Co., levistrauss.com/
- "Front Loading Washers," Consumer Search, consumersearch.com/washing-machine-reviews/front-loading-washers
- "The Green Guide," National Geographic, environment.nationalgeographic.com/environment/green-guide/?source=NavEnvGG
- "Clothes Washers: Buyer's Guide," Energy Star, energystar.gov/index.cfm?c=clotheswash.pr_tips_clothes_washers

3. Get Shower Power
- "Water Science for Schools," US Geological Study, ga.water.usgs.gov/edu/
- "Experts Fear Much of US Could Face Water Shortage," Associated Press, October 27, 2007, foxnews.com/story/0,2933,305578,00.html
- "Save Money in the Shower," The Daily Green, thedailygreen.com/going-green/community-tips/shorter-showers-save-water
- "What You Can Do: Use Your WaterSense!" UN Environmental Protection Agency, epa.gov/WaterSense/water_efficiency/what_you_can_do.html
- National Geographic, Water Conservation "Water Conservation Tips," National

Geographic, environment.nationalgeographic.com/environment/freshwater/water-conservation-tips/

4. Color Your Hair Green

- Wu, Jessica, "A Natural Alternative to Chemical Hair Dyes," Daily Glow, September 25, 2009, dailyglow.com/hair-care-tips/a-natural-alternative-to-chemical-hair-dyes.html
- Millennium Ecosystem Assessment. Ecosystems and Human Well-Being: Current State and Trends: Findings of the Condition and Trends Working Group (Island Press, US, 2005), 431.
- Modric, Jan, "Hair Dye Allergies," Health Hype, healthhype.com/hair-dye-allergies.html
- Cathy, "Homemade Hair Dyes," Green Eco Services (blog), November 5, 2008, greenecoservices.com/homemade-hair-dyes/
- "Henna Hair Dyes," Lush, lushusa.com/shop/products/haircare/henna-hair-dyes/
- "iRecycle," Earth911.com, earth911.com/irecycle/
- "Household Hazardous Waste Facility," Recology Sunset Scavenger, sunsetscavenger.com/hazardousWasteFacility.htm
- Aveda, aveda.com/

5. Be a Natural Beauty

- "Pots of Promise," The Economist, May 22, 2003, economist.com/node/1795852?story_id=1795852
- Rogers, Elizabeth and Kostigen, Thomas M., The Green Book: The Everyday Guide to Saving the Planet One Simple Step at a Time. New York: Three Rivers Press, 2007, 101.
- Heller, Lorraine, " 'Natural' Will Remain Undefined, Says FDA," Food Navigator-USA, foodnavigator-usa.com/Financial-Industry/Natural-will-remain-undefined-says-FDA
- "Cosmetics," US Food and Drug Administration, fda.gov/Cosmetics/default.htm
- Energy Kids, eia.doe.gov/kids/
- Drugstore.com, drugstore.com
- "Human Taxome Project," Environmental Working Group, ewg.org/
- Gonzalez, Helena, "Sunscreen with Benzophenone-3 Unsuitable for Children," Medical News Today, November 10, 2006, medicalnewstoday.com/releases/56091.php
- "21 of the Best Natural Sunscreens," The Daily Green, thedailygreen.com/environmental-news/latest/natural-sunscreens-460608
- The Refill Shoppe, therefillshoppe.com/
- "The Compact for Safe Cosmetics," The Campaign for Safe Cosmetics, safecosmetics.org/section.php?id=51
- Koerner, Brendan, "Wear Green, Drink Greenly: The Eco-Guide to Responsible Drinking," Slate, March 16, 2009, slate.com/id/2186219/
- *Technology Special Interest Quarterly, American Occupation Therapy Association (Vol. 279 No. 2), March 2007 – April 2007*
- "Antiperspirants/Deodorants and Breast Cancer: Questions and Answers," National Cancer Institute, cancer.gov/cancertopics/factsheet/Risk/AP-Deo
- Crystal Deodorant Protection, crystaldeodorantprotection.com/

6. Bark Up the Right Tree

- Natural Environmental Satellite, Data, and Information Service, nesdis.noaa.gov/
- Seward, Elizabeth, "How Long Will Your

Clothes Live in a Landfill," Planet Green, March 4, 2009, planetgreen.discovery.com/fashion-beauty/clothes-live-landfill.html

- Earth Dog: Quality Hemp Products for Dogs, earthdog.com/
- BioBag, biobagusa.com/
- "Nitrous Oxide: Sources and Emissions," US EPA, epa.gov/nitrousoxide/sources.html
- De Vito, Dominique, Green Dog, Good Dog: Reducing Your Best Friend's Carbon Paw Print, Asheville, North Carolina: Lark Books, 2009

7. Have a Green Christmas

- "Winter Tips," US EPA, epa.gov/epahome/hi-winter.htm
- National Christmas Tree Association, christmastree.org/
- Mezensky, Catherine, "Adding a Potted Christmas Tree to Your Holiday Décor, *Baltimore Examiner*, December 2, 2009, examiner.com/gardening-in-baltimore/adding-a-potted-christmas-tree-to-your-holiday-d-cor
- "How Christmas Tree Rental Works," The Living Christmas Co., livingchristmas.com/info/tree/how.php
- Fehrenbacher, Jill, "How To: Green Your Christmas Tree," Inhabitat, December 18, 2010, inhabitat.com/how-to-green-your-christmas-tree/
- "LED Holiday Lights," Greenhome.com, greenhome.com/products/lighting/led_holiday_lights/

8. Greenify Your House

- "Draft Dodger," Martha Stewart, marthastewart.com/265344/draft-dodger
- "Compact Fluorescent Light Bulbs," Light Bulbs Etc., Inc, lightbulbsdirect.com/page/001/CTGY/CompactFluorescent
- Diaz, Kevin, "Bachmann Is Pro-Choice on Bulbs," Star Tribune, March 26, 2008, tartribune.com/politics/statelocal/17002506.html
- "IKEA Pulls the Plug on All Incandescent Light Bulbs," Business Wire, January 4, 2011, businesswire.com/news/home/20110104005336/en/IKEA-Pulls-Plug-Incandescent-Light-Bulbs
- Formisano, Bob, "2007 Energy Bill—Are They Phasing Out or Making Incandescent Bulbs Illegal?" About.com, homerepair.about.com/od/electricalrepair/ss/2007_energybill.htm
- "Toilet Tank Bank," Earth Easy, eartheasy.com/toilet-tank-bank
- "The Home Depot," iTunes Preview, itunes.apple.com/us/app/the-home-depot/id342527639?mt=8

10. Eat Your Greens

- "Rearing Cattle Produces More Greenhouse Gases than Driving Cars, UN Report Warns," UN News Center, November 29, 2006, un.org/apps/news/story.asp?newsID=20772&CR1=warning
- "Livestock Industry and Global Warming," Green Planet Awards, greenplanetawards.org/livestock.html
- "Ruminant Livestock," US EPA, epa.gov/rlep/
- Arkisaeo, "Livestock vs. Transportation: Which Is really Worse?" Greenfudge (blog), March 28, 2010, greenfudge.org/2010/03/28/livestock-vs-transportation-which-is-really-worse/
- Agriculture and Consumer Protection, Livestock's Long Shadow (Agriculture and

Consumer Protection, United Nations, 2006)
- "The Better Crocker Cookbook for iPhone and iPod Touch Devices," Better Crocker, bettycrocker.com/mobilecookbook/default

11. Put Down the Bottle
- "Tap Water Quality and Safety," Natural Resources Defense Council, nrdc.org/water/drinking/qtap.asp
- "Bottled Water Costs Consumers and the Environment," Food & Water Watch, foodandwaterwatch.org/water/bottled/bottled-water-bad-for-people-and-the-environment/
- "Bottled Water Market Share Volume Holds Steady in 2009 Despite Poor Economic Conditions," International Bottled Water Association, May 13, 2010, bottledwater.org/news/bottled-water-market-share-volume-holds-steady-2009-despite-poor-economic-conditions
- Refill Not Landfill, refillnotlandfill.org/
- "The Story of Bottled Water," The Story of Stuff Project, storyofstuff.org/bottledwater/
- "Aquafina Labels to Spell Out Source—Tap Water," CNN.com, Just 27, 2007, cnn.com/2007/HEALTH/07/27/pepsico.aquafina.reut/
- Mui, Ylan Q., "Bottled Water Sales See a Drought," Los Angeles Times, August 14, 2009, articles.latimes.com/2009/aug/14/business/fi-water14
- "Since You Asked—Bisphenol A (BPA)," National Institute of Environmental Health Sciences—National Institutes of Health, niehs.nih.gov/news/media/questions/sya-bpa.cfm
- "Frequently Asked Questions," Klean Kanteen, kleankanteen.com/faqs/faqs.php
- "Disposable Water Bottle Alternatives," Earth911.com, earth911.com/news/2008/06/02/disposable-water-bottle-alternatives/

12. Check Your Carbon Footprint
- "Become Carbon Neutral," Climate Crisis, climatecrisis.net/take_action/become_carbon_neutral.php
- What's My Carbon Footprint? whatsmycarbonfootprint.com
- TerraPass.com *terrapass.com*
- Zero Footprint Challenge, usa.zerochallenge.org//challenge

13. Cans, Bottles, Paper, What?
- "Municipal Solid Waste in the United States: Facts and Figures 2009," US EPA, December 2010, epa.gov/osw/nonhaz/municipal/msw99.htm
- "Why Are Plastic Bags So Bad for Your Recycling Bin," PlanetArk, recyclingweek.planetark.org/recycling-info/plasticbags.cfm
- PlasticBagRecycling.org, plasticbagrecycling.org/plasticbag/index.html
- "The Nuts and Bolts of Recycling," Do It Green, doitgreen.org/article/home/recycling
- Glass Packaging Institute, gpi.org
- "What Happens Next to Plastic Bags," Earth911.com, earth911.com
- "Recycle Your Sneakers: Nike Creates Playground with Your Old Shoes!" Blue Egg, blueegg.com
- "The 'Battery Act,'" *Enforcement Alert*, US EPA, Vol. 5, No. 2. March 2002, epa.gov/oecaerth/resources/newsletters/civil/enfalert/battery.pdf
- Dermody, K.C., "How to Recycle Batteries," *Associate Content*. December 7, 2010, associ-

atedcontent.com/article/6091842/how_to_re-cycle_batteries.html
- "Now Accepting #1-7 Plastic Bottles, Tubs and Jars in Your Curbside Recycling Bin!" Eco Cycle, ecocycle.org/guidelines/plastics/index.cfm
- "Preserve, Gimme 5," Preserve Products, preserveproducts.com/recycling/gimme5.html

14. Don't Toss That!
- "*Garbage Dreams* – Recycling," PBS.org: Independent Lens, pbs.org/independentlens/garbage-dreams/recycling.html
- "Municipal Solid Wastes," US EPA, epa.gov/epawaste/nonhaz/municipal/index.htm
- Recycle.co.uk, recycle.co.uk

15. Let No French Fry Go to Waste
- "Food Waste Management Cost Calculator,"US EPA, epa.gov/osw/conserve/materials/organics/food/tools/
- "California Recycling Laws," Californians Against Waste, cawrecycles.org/facts_and_stats/california_recycling_laws
- *School Composting, A Manual for Connecticut Schools*, Connecticut Department of Environmental Protection Recycling Program, cawrecycles.org/facts_and_stats/california_recycling_laws
- "Composting," US EPA, Composting, epa.gov/epawaste/conserve/rrr/composting/index.htm

16. Get the Right Stuff
- "Choose an Environmentally Friendly Backpack,"*The Green Your Blog*, greenyour.com/lifestyle/leisure-recreation/camping-gear/tips/choose-an-environmentally-friendly-backpack

- "The Poison Plastic," Greenpeace, greenpeace.org/international/en/campaigns/toxics/polyvinyl-chloride/the-poison-plastic/
- "Recycling By the Numbers," Green Living Tips, greenlivingtips.com/articles/187/1/Recycling-by-the-numbers.html
- Abdollah, Tami, "That 'new shower curtain smell'? It's toxic, study says," *LA Times*. June 13, 2008. articles.latimes.com/2008/jun/13/local/me-showercurtain13
- "Summary of the Resource Conservation and Recovery Act," US EPA, epa.gov/regulations/laws/rcra.html
- "What is Post-Consumer Recycled Content?" *Metro*, oregonmetro.gov/index.cfm/go/by.web/id=3369

17. Cut to the Paper Chase
- "How Paper is Made," Idaho Forest Products Commission, idahoforests.org/papr-make.htm
- TAPPI Paper University, tappi.org
- "A Shopper's Guide to Home Tissue Products," Natural Resources Defense Council (NRDC), nrdc.org/land/forests/gtissue.asp
- *Green Teacher's Guide, Miami Herald*, nie.miamiherald.com/_pdf/NIEGreenTeachers-Guide1.pdf
- *Teach English, Teach About the Enviornment,* US EPA, September 2007, epa.gov/osw/education/pdfs/tesol.pdf
- Oberlin College Resource Conversation Team, new.oberlin.edu/office/facilities-operations/recycle/links.dot
- "Solid Waste Management," Bergen County, Utilities Authority, bcua.org/SolidWaste.htm
- The Paper Mill Store, thepapermillstore.com

18. Paint the Halls Green

- Precita Eyes Muralists, precitaeyes.org
- City of Philadelphia, Mural Arts Program, muralarts.org

19. Take It To the Top

- "Schools: An Overview of Energy Use and Energy Efficiency Opportunities," Energy Star, energystar.gov/ia/business/challenge/learn_more/Schools.pdf
- "Common Questions about Energy-Efficiency Projects," Missouri Department of Natural Resources, dnr.mo.gov/pubs/pub1465.pdf
- "Energy Savers," US Department of Energy, energysavers.gov/

20. Feel the (Solar) Power

- American Energy Independence, americanenergyindependence.com
- "Solar Energy is the Best Alternative," Green and Simple Living, green-and-simple-living.com/solar-energy.html
- Encyclopedia Britannica Online, s.v. "Solar Cell," britannica.com/EBchecked/topic/552875/solar-cell
- Renewable Energy World, renewableenergyworld.com
- Encyclopedia Britannica Online, s.v. "Charles Fritts," britannica.com/EBchecked/topic/220537/Charles-Fritts
- "Renewable Energy Sources in the United States," NationalAtlas.gov, nationalatlas.gov/articles/people/a_energy.html
- Solio: solar chargers, solio.com/chargers/
- Voltaic, voltaicsystems.com
- Bloch, Michael, "Recycling Disposable or Rechargeable Batteries," Green Living Tips, November 18, 2006, greenlivingtips.com/articles/12/1/Recycling-disposable-or-rechargeable-batteries.html
- "FAQs GreenBatteries.com, greenbatteries.com
- Romm, Joseph, "The Technology that Will Save Humanity," *Salon*, April 14, 2008, salon.com/news/feature/2008/04/14/solar_electric_thermal
- "Solar Energy History," Solar Home, solar-home.org/infosolarenergyhistory.html
- "Solar Technology," New Generation Power, newgenerationpower.org/about-solar/solar-technology/

21. Save Your Cell

- Lenhart, Amanda, "Teens and Mobile Phones," Pew Internet Project, April 20, 2010, pewinternet.org/Reports/2010/Teens-and-Mobile-Phones.aspx
- "National Study Reveals How Teens are Shaping & Reshaping Their Wireless World. Study Sheds New Light On Teens' Cell Phone Habits, Expectations & Dream Phone Wishes,"CTIA, September 12, 2008, ctia.org/media/press/body.cfm/prid/1774
- "Fact Sheet: Recycle Your Cell Phone. It's An Easy Call." US EPA, February 2009, epa.gov/osw/partnerships/plugin/cellphone/cell-fs.htm
- Recellular, recellular.com
- "Plug-In to eCycling," US EPA, epa.gov/osw/partnerships/plugin/
- Cell Phones For Soldiers, cellphonesforsoldiers.com
- "The Electronic Wasteland," *60 Minutes*, November 18, 2008, CBSnews.com

22. Compute the Difference

- "How to Reduce Your Energy Consumption," National Resources Defense Council (NRDC), nrdc.org/air/energy/genergy/simple.asp
- "Computers for Consumers," Energy Star, energystar.gov/index.cfm?fuseaction=find_a_product.showProductGroup&pgw_code=CO
- "Looking for a New Computer? Choose a Laptop Over a Desktop," Green Living Works! greenlivingworks.com/looking-for-a-new-computer-choose-a-laptop-over-a-desktop/26
- "Energy Savers," US Department of Energy, energysavers.gov
- "Is Your Home a "Green" House?" *National Geographic Magazine*, nationalgeographic.com/everyday/greenhouse/index.html

23. Rewind and Unplug

- "Suggested Content for the Benefits of Your Energy Star Qualified Product," Energy Star, energystar.gov/index.cfm?c=manuf_res.web_based_tools_prodspec
- "Home Tips," Energy Star, energystar.gov/index.cfm?c=products.es_at_home_tips
- "Smart Power Strips," Tree Hugger, treehugger.com/files/2005/12/smart_power_str.php
- "Let's Pull the Plug on Energy Waste," Nokia nokia.com/environment/devices-and-services/energy-effiency
- Pressnell, Josh, "Battery Alert!" iTunes Preview, itunes.apple.com/us/app/battery-alert/id416283462?mt=8

24. BYOB (Bring Your Own Bag)

- Conway, Chris, "Taking Aim at All Those Plastic Bags," *The New York Times*, April 1, 2007, nytimes.com/2007/04/01/weekinreview/01basics.html
- "Disadvantages of Using Plastic Bags," LiveStrong.com, livestrong.com/article/156070-disadvantages-of-using-plastic-bags/

25. Go Vintage

- "Consumer Expenditure Survey," US Bureau of Labor Statistics, October, 2010, bls.gov/cex/
- "Polyester," Encyclopedia.com, encyclopedia.com/topic/polyester.aspx
- "Textiles and the Environment," Instyle, instyle.com.au/sustainable.html
- Claudio, Luz, "Waste Couture: Environmental Impact of the Clothing Industry," Environmental Health Perspectives, September 2007, ncbi.nlm.nih.gov/pmc/articles/PMC1964887/

26. Buy Green Threads

- "Bedding," *The GreenYour Blog*, greenyour.com/home.bedroom/bedding
- Editors of Green Guide. *Green Guide: The Complete Reference for Consuming Wisely* (National Geographic, US, 2008), 220.
- Mikee Mercader, "The Health and Environmental Problems with Clothes Dyes," Cottonique (blog), September 2, 2010, cottonique.com/blogs/blog/1943892-the-health-and-environmental-problems-with-clothes-dyes
- "Agriculture and Environment: Cotton," WWF, wwf.panda.org/what_we_do/footprint/agriculture/cotton/better_management_practices/
- "Go Green Gina: Top Natural Fabric Dyes," J&O Fabrics Store Newsletter Blog, July 27,

2010, jandofabrics.com/newsletters/go-green-gina-top-natural-fabric-dyes/

- "Natural & Plant Dyes," Aurora Silk, aurorasilk.com/natural_dyes/dyes/index.html
- "Fabrics: E-Fibers," Patagonia, patagonia.com/us/patagonia.go?assetid=10097
- "Organic Cotton Facts," Organic Trade Association, ota.com/organic/mt/organic_cotton.html
- Rosenthal, Elisabeth, "Can Polyester Save the World?" *The New York Times*, January 25, 2007, nytimes.com/2007/01/25/fashion/25pollute.html

27. Give Green

- "Men's Shoes," Greenzer, greenzer.com/mens-shoes_8_28
- Flat Tire Footwear, lattirefootwear.com/#/Home
- Saad, Lydia, "Consumers Issue a Cautious Christmas Spending Forecast,"Gallup, October 25, 2010. gallup.com/poll/143987/consumers-issue-cautious-christmas-spending-forecast.aspx
- "2010 Christmas Gift Spending Plans Jump," American Research Group, Inc, November 22, 2010, americanresearchgroup.com/holiday/
- "The GiveNow Card," JustGive, justgive.org/give-now/gift-cards/index.jsp
- "Give a Charity Gift Card," Give Now Cards, charitynavigator.org/index.cfm?bay=content.view&cpid=699
- "Eco Gift Wrap," Martha Stewart, marthastewart.com/270379/eco-gift-wrap

28. Keep It Local

- "What Is Local?" Sustainable Table, marthastewart.com/270379/eco-gift-wrap
- Local Harvest, localharvest.org/
- FoodRoutes, foodroutes.org/

29. Go Organic

- Organic.org, organic.org/
"Nutrition Labeling, Facility Consultant,
- Label Expeditor and more..." USDA-FDA, organic.org/
- "National Organic Program," USDA, ams.usda.gov/AMSv1.0/nop
- The European Commission of Agriculture and Rural Development, ec.europa.eu/agriculture/
- University of California, Agriculture and Natural Resources, ucanr.org/
- "What is Organic?" The Natural Organic Program, ams.usda.gov/AMSv1.0/NOP
- "Organic Cotton Facts," Organic Trade Association, ota.com/organic/mt/organic_cotton.html
- "Organic Food Labeling," Green Living Tips, July 7, 2009, greenlivingtips.com/categories/food/

30. Tune It Up

- US Department of Energy, Energy Efficiency and Renewable Energy, eere.energy.gov/
- "Energy Efficiency Advice From Alliance to Save Energy," Sustainable City Network, January 9, 2011, sustainablecitynetwork.com/topic_channels/energy/article_86ebf34a-1c56-11e0-9840-00127992bc8b.html
- "Keeping Your Car In Shape," US Department of Energy, fueleconomy.gov/feg/maintain.shtml

- "Fuel Economy: Getting Up to Speed," Federal Trade Commission, ftc.gov/bcp/edu/microsites/energysavings/garage.htm

31. Turn it Off

- Georgia Department of Transportation, dot.state.ga.us/Pages/default.aspx
- "Tips to Save Gas and Improve Mileage," US EPA, epa.gov/oms/consumer/17-tips.pdf
- Stevens, Melissa, "Turn Off that Car and Stop Polluting," *The Tennessean*, February 21, 2010, cleanairpartnership.info/Media%20Room/TurnOffThatCarAndStop-Polluting.pdf
- "Your Car and Clean Air: What YOU Can Do to Reduce Pollution," US Environmental Protection Agency, epa.gov/oms/consumer/18-youdo.pdf
- Brown, Chris, "Water Conservation in the Professional Car Wash Industry," International Carwash Association, 2000, google.com/search?sourceid=chrome&ie=UTF-8&q=water+conservation+in+the+professional+car+wash+industry+brown
- Lacko, Rebecca, "Green Living 101: The Eco-Friendly Car Wash," *The National Examiner*, August 18, 2009, examiner.com/green-living-in-national/green-living-101-the-eco-friendly-car-wash
- "Give Your Car an Eco-Friendly Car Wash," *The GreenYour Blog*, greenyour.com/transportation/car/car-driving/tips/give-your-car-an-eco-friendly-wash

32. Jump in the Pool

- California Environmental Protection Agency, Air Resources Board, arb.ca.gov/homepage.htm
- "Mobile Source Emissions—Past, Present and Future," US EPA, epa.gov/otaq/invntory/overview/
- "Research Library," Golden Gate Bridge, goldengatebridge.org/research/
- Starr, Adam, "Carpooling Quietly Booms in San Francisco," *Good Magazine*, February 7, 2009, good.is/post/carpooling-quietly-booms-in-san-francisco/
- "Drive More Efficiently," US Department of Energy, fueleconomy.gov/feg/drivehabits.shtml

33. Go On An Eco-Adventure

- "Ecotourism Resource Center," EcoTour, ecotourdirectory.com/ecotourism/
- National Outdoor Leadership School, nols.edu/
- "Scholarship Policies," Outward Bound, outwardbound.org/index.cfm/do/exp.scholarship_policies
- "Student Opportunities," Earthwatch Institute, arthwatch.org/studentopp

34. Be a Green Guest

- Streeter, A. K., "Albuquerque Hotel Cuts Water Use Nearly 80%," *Tree Hugger*, July 22, 2010, treehugger.com/files/2010/07/leed-gold-hotel-cuts-water-use-significantly.php
- University of Florida, Treeo Center, treeo.ufl.edu/
- Klaus Reichardt, "Measure Your Hotel's Water Consumption, Then Start Saving," 4Hoteliers, February 18 2007, 4hoteliers.com/4hots_fshw.php?mwi=1889
- "Industry Statistics Sampler: Hotels (Except Casino Hotels) and Motels," US Census Bureau, March 4, 2011, census.gov/econ/

industry/current/c721110.htm

- "Plunkett's Travel Airline, Hotel & Travel Industry," Plunkett Research Ltd., plunkettresearch.com/travel%20tourism%20market%20research/industry%20and%20business%20data
- "The Green Plan for Hotels," NC Division of Pollution Prevention and Environmental Assistance, p2pays.org/hospitality/
- Alliance for Water Efficiency, a4we.org/
- Sustainability Committee, American Public University System, apus-sustainability.com/
- Lawrence Berkeley National Laboratory, lbl.gov/
- Madison Gas and Electric, mge.com/

39. Order the Green Plate Special
- "Basic Information About Food Waste," US EPA, mge.com/
- "Facts at a Glance," National Restaurant Association, restaurant.org/research/facts/

40. Throw A Party Green-Style
- "A Shopper's Guide to Home Tissue Products," Natural Resources Defense Council (NRDC), nrdc.org/land/forests/gtissue.asp
- "Chlorine," Chemistry Explained, chemistry-explained.com/elements/A-C/Chlorine.html
- "Environmental Concerns in the Paper Making Process," Paper Industry, paperindustry.com/environmental-concerns.asp

41. Get Greens for Greening
- Becky Bones, beckybones.com/Home/tab-id/36/Default.aspx

42. Turn Free Time Into Green Time
- Cellular Nutrition, acu-cell.com/
- Volunteer Match, volunteermatch.org/
- Planet Connect, planet-connect.org/
/

43. Yours Treely
- "Benefits of Trees in Urban Areas," Colorado Tree Coalition, coloradotrees.org/benefits.htm
- "Why Buy Real Christmas Trees," Christmas Tree Farm Network, christmas-tree.com/real/realchristmastrees.html
- Johnson, Hollan, "Effects of Plants on Air Pollution," Garden Guides, gardenguides.com/86160-effects-plants-air-pollution.html
- Galveston-Houston Association for Smog Prevention (GHASP), Trees & Our Air (GHASP, US, 1999)
- "What Is Ozone," US EPA, epa.gov/airnow/airaware/day1-ozone.html
- Trees for the Future, plant-trees.org/

44. Get Growing
- Pounders, Sarah, "Starting a Community Garden on School Grounds," Kids Gardening, 2011, kidsgardening.com/Dig/digdetail.taf?Type=Art&id=2222
- Surls, Rachel, Community Garden Start-Up Guide, UC Cooperative Extension County, Updated March 2001

46. Get Political
- "Resources," Student World Assembly, studentworldassembly.org/category.php?slug=/category/resources/
- Act MTV, act.mtv.com/
- TeenActivist.Org, teenactivist.org/

About the Author

Photo by Liz Lopez

Lexi Petronis has written articles about health, nutrition, the environment, news and more for magazines such as *CosmoGIRL!*, *Glamour*, and *Fitness*. She's also the editor-in-chief of *Albuquerque The Magazine*, and lives in Albuquerque, New Mexico with her husband and daughter.

Acknowledgments

Special thanks to those who made this book come to life: the amazingly smart, creative, talented team at Zest, including Karen Macklin, Nikki Roddy, and Hallie Warshaw; my always-supportive and encouraging husband, David; and my children, Rowan Beth and River Samuel, who are beautiful, constant reminders about the importance of taking care of our planet.

Other Zest Books

97 Things to Do Before You Finish High School
by Steven Jenkins and Karen Macklin

87 Ways to Throw a Killer Party
by Melissa Daly

How to Fight, Lie, and Cry Your Way to Popularity (and a Prom Date)
Lousy Life Lessons from 50 Teen Movies
by Nikki Roddy

Scandalous!
50 Shocking Events You Should Know About
(So You Can Impress Your Friends)
by Hallie Fryd

Indie Girl
From Starting a Band to Launching a Fashion Company, Nine Ways to
Turn Your Creative Talent into Reality
by Arne Johnson and Karen Macklin

Girls Against Girls
Why We Are Mean to Each Other and How We Can Change
by Bonnie Burton